Bus Driver Diaries

Stories From the Driver's Seat

Tory C Anderson

Published by Oryander Publishing
PO Box 445 Levan UT 84639

ISBN-10: 1519558724
ISBN-13: 978-1519558725

DEDICATION

To the moment I realized I was not a normal man pretending to be an artist, but an artist pretending to be a normal man.

CONTENTS

ACKNOWLEDGMENTS

To the beautiful kids who have ridden, are currently riding, and who will ride my bus—I love you even when I'm yelling *Sit down and be quiet!* To my wife who quietly reads my chapters and gives me valuable feedback—I am deeply appreciative. Thank you to my revision editor, Lisa Rubilar, whose red ink and encouragement work wonders with my words. A special thanks to my copy editor, Eva Call, who helps me go to press feeling confident.

PREFACE

OR

HOW SIX YEARS OF COLLEGE LANDED ME A JOB AS A SCHOOL BUS DRIVER

A yellow school bus is as iconic as a church steeple or the American flag. The sight of a school bus, in life or in pictures, immediately invokes memories of school and friends. I rode the bus to school only one year, in eighth grade. That was because the Burley Junior High burned to the ground and they shipped the entire class ten miles to Declo. There we attended an ancient, condemned school house while they built the new Burley Junior High. I have many mundane memories of all those rides out and back again—all of them forever framed in the yellow and black of a school bus.

My most memorable bus ride came on a trip with the band. There, near the back, during a game of Truth or Dare, I experienced my first kiss. The noise of the tires, the chatter of the other kids, the darkness between the middle seat where kids hung over from front and back to be in the game, the butterflies, the softness of lips—that bus ride lingers with me still. Other than the kiss I had little emotional investment in school buses. There was nothing to prepare me for the day I would find myself the captain of one.

Although driving a school bus never occurred to me in my wildest dreams, perhaps it was inevitable. The likelihood of driving a bus goes up for a kid who graduates from college still not knowing what he wants to be. My first degree was a BA in English. There was nothing casual about my choosing to major in English. I entered college with the dream of becoming an astronomer. I had grown up reading science fiction and felt an affinity for space and the stars. After three attempts at Math 1010 ended in failure I finally realized that science wasn't in my future. During this same period of time I discovered the Arts and Humanities. Moving from astronomy to the arts made sense, when I thought about it years later. It wasn't the cold, mathematics of astronomy that attracted me, but the stories of space written by intelligent creative writers such as Ray Bradbury and Isaac Asimov. From astronomy I made the long leap to acting; from acting to playwriting; and from playwriting finally to English. Landing as an English major was a victory in my life. The major encompassed philosophy, history, psychology, critical thinking and so much more, all through literature. Ironically, finding my home in the English Department didn't help me know what I wanted to be when I grew up. What do you do with an English degree? The answer to that is *anything you want,* but I didn't know that at the time.

When I graduated with my BA I still had no idea what to do for a career. That wasn't because English is a poor life choice, but because the idea of getting a job was such a letdown after years of journeying through literature and ideas. I temporarily solved the problem by going back to school.

I was working at the Humanities reference desk in the campus library when I graduated with my BA. I naturally looked into the master's program in English, first. I was intimidated by the fact that in order to graduate candidates were required to take oral exams and successfully defend a thesis. I still didn't have that kind of confidence. After consulting with two different English professors, one then a librarian, I chose the master of library and information systems route. After all, I needed to face the fact that one day I had to get a job. Both professors assured me that being a librarian was a much more practical career route.

Six months later I was so miserable in the program that I couldn't withstand English's siren song. I overcame the intimidation and, against the advice of three professors, I entered the English master's program at BYU. What followed were the best two years of my life.

It was then I discovered creative writing. Finally I knew what I wanted to be—a writer. This discovery changed my life, but not as immediately as I wished. My desire was deep and genuine, but my understanding of what it meant to be a writer was at the same level as a punk who wants to be a Marine. The punk can only imagine mowing down enemy soldiers with a machine gun and throwing hand grenades. He isn't ready for the pushups, the verbal abuse, the forced fifty-mile hikes. I wasn't ready for the ambiguity that comes with being a writer.

When I graduated with my MA I had a wife and three children. They needed to eat. I could write all right, but no one wanted to pay me to do it—unless it was technical writing. An aspiring novelist looks upon technical writing with as much enthusiasm as his turn at cleaning the toilet. Still, I accepted a position as a technical writer for a high tech company in order to be a responsible husband and father. After I got over my bad attitude I found the job to be a pleasant surprise. The company culture was positive. I made a good salary with benefits. I rose from technical writing to become director of training and technical services. Eventually I became a technical sales consultant and traveled around the world. Finding myself in Rio de Janeiro, Istanbul, and Rome, among many other foreign lands, surprised me as much as, later, finding myself a bus driver.

In spite of the wonderful fifteen years I had with that company I never felt totally at ease while there. For reasons I didn't understand I always felt a bit of a pretender in the corporate business and high tech worlds. Perhaps that's why, when the company hit a dead end, so had I. When I was laid off, along with almost everyone else, I was so burned out that I wanted nothing more to do with corporate business. The thought of getting another similar job turned my stomach. The problem was that, by then, I had eight children. They had grown accustomed to eating and liked the idea of living in a house. I needed to find a way to take care of them.

It was 2008 and the great recession was just beginning. People everywhere were losing their jobs. In desperation I opened a computer repair shop. This was another surprise in my life. It's interesting what an education in the Humanities enables a person to do. My liberal arts education didn't include training in class four tandem switching platforms which were what my previous job centered around, or running a business in computer repair, and yet it made me capable of success in both areas. This is because a liberal arts degree gave me the ability to think, to adapt, and to keep learning. My experience as a ham radio operator as a youth and later as a radar technician in the Air National Guard helped, too.

Computer repair proved an interesting and valuable experience for eight years. But as the cost of computers declined so did the profitability of computer repair. It became clear that I needed to find something to augment my income. A bus driving acquaintance informed me that there was an opening in the district force.

I can't tell you how strange it felt to find myself interviewing to be a school bus driver. Driving a school bus wasn't for middle-aged, college educated men like me. School bus driving was for retired men, or for women who were bored or who needed more disposable income. I had to ask myself a difficult question—was I giving up on my life by choosing to become a school bus driver?

I might have turned my back on the job if my desire to write hadn't come out of hibernation at this time. During the fifteen years of my traditional job I was too comfortable to write. Running a one-man computer repair shop in a small town was not comfortable. My family was living far below the poverty line. The financial stress opened up cracks in the shell around my soul that let the creative juices start to flow again. It occurred to me that accepting a job as a school bus driver would help feed the family while allowing those creative juices to keep flowing. Being a school bus driver wasn't a sign that I was a loser; it was an enabling opportunity to be what I was born to be: a writer.

Becoming a school bus driver has turned out to be much more than a tool to enable me to write. It has actively fueled my inspiration to write. A bus driver is tossed into a sea of humanity. The kids who ride the bus have two separate lives: home life and school life. The school bus is the bridge between these two worlds. It is, in fact, a third world that only the bus driver witnesses. I had no idea of the powerful flashes of life I would see as these kids got on and off the bus. I didn't know a person could build meaningful relationships on such brief encounters. These relationships are unique because they are made of moments. These short vignettes aim at capturing the moments in that third world.

NOTE: *Like many school bus drivers I began as a substitute driver. Substituting is a unique experience that will put any human being out of his comfort zone and, in many ways, is quite different from having a regular route. I substituted for six months before being assigned a regular route. The first seven chapters describe my substitute experience.*

1 - JUST A ROOKIE

Being a school bus driver is not a thing most people aspire to. I certainly didn't. Never in my life did I wake up and think, "I'd like to be a school bus driver." And yet here I am in the pilot seat of one of those long, yellow machines. It's only been a short time and already I am beginning to see that being a school bus driver isn't just a job—it's an opportunity and an adventure. The opportunity lies in suddenly finding myself a part of so many other people's lives: the other bus drivers, the kids, the teachers, and even the parents. As for the adventure, picture this: eighty-four kids on a bus, some are bullies, some are sweet, some are sick (throw-up variety), some are exuberant, some are sad . . . You get the picture.

Being the new bus driver makes me a rookie. The other bus drivers, almost all of them ladies, have been driving between ten and twenty-five years. They are veterans. Blizzards, heat waves, mechanical breakdowns far from home, sick students—they've seen it all. I worry about the day that something unforeseen is going to happen on my bus. Will I be able to handle it appropriately?

The other day I was doing the afternoon pickup at the high school. There was a line of buses in front of me in the usual order. As the buses finished loading and began to roll, one of the veteran drivers radioed me.

"Tory, can you follow me to Perkins today? I've got a feeling this bus isn't going to make it."

I wondered what that was about. My bus followed her bus to Perkins every night anyway, but I told her I would. Perkins is a very

5

small town thirteen miles south of the high school. It may be small, but lots of children live there. Every morning three busloads of kids are brought to the High School and elementary schools located in the city, and every night the same buses take the kids back to Perkins.

Just outside of the city the highway narrows as it climbs a ridge. I was a quarter-mile behind the veteran's bus and slowly gaining on her. At a distance I noticed her bus was leaving an unusual amount of diesel fumes behind. As I got closer I smelled, not diesel, but burning brakes. I could see smoke pouring out of her right, rear tire well. This looked serious to me. I radioed her and explained what I saw. The highway to Perkins is well-maintained, but it has no shoulder whatsoever. Instead there is a steep embankment that could roll a bus. Stopping a busload of kids in the middle of the highway would be dangerous. I wondered what she was going to do.

"Okay," she said, calmly. "I'll pull off at the IFA road. You follow me."

I had forgotten about the junction to the Intermountain Farmers Association feed processing facility. At the IFA junction a few miles further along the highway widens just enough for a turnout lane for trucks hauling feed. Her bus would clog the turnout lane, but it wasn't used all that much and her bus would be to the side of the main traffic. When we finally reached it she pulled off. I followed, still not knowing what she was going to do after she stopped. As I waited for further instructions the third Perkins bus pulled in unannounced behind me. The driver was another veteran.

"Tory, send all your west-side kids to me," she said over the radio.

My kids were going crazy with the excitement of an unexpected stop and I couldn't make out what she meant. Some of my kids heard and understood. Without any prompting from me I noticed a third of my kids lined up in the aisle and then filed off my bus. In my passenger side mirrors I watched them walk back and get on the other bus that had called for my west-side kids. No sooner was the last west-side kid off when I saw a line of kids from the bus in front of me queuing up outside my door. They loaded onto my bus in an orderly fashion taking the seats that were left vacant by the west-side kids who had just left. With my west-side kids onboard the bus behind me left for Perkins. A few minutes later I followed. As I pulled away from the turning lane I glanced in my rearview mirror and saw a state trooper pulling in behind the disabled bus. The driver had called for a trooper in case there was a need for traffic control. I also heard that a tow truck was already on the way to pick up the driver and the bus.

In town I had to drop off kids from two different routes. I knew one of the routes but was at a loss for the other one. I stopped at an intersection and sat trying to map a route in my head. A high school student, sensing my dilemma, came to the front of the bus, sat in the seat near mine, and guided me to each stop.

After the last student got off I sat amazed at how smoothly the whole situation had been resolved. The first driver sensed there was going to be trouble and made sure I was going to be there to help. The third driver, when she heard our chatter on the radio, instinctively knew that the kids from the first bus would be transferring to my bus. This was going to make me overcrowded. Needing no instructions she stopped and took the students from the west side of town that were closest to her route. What could have been a very disruptive situation was kept a minor incident by the professionalism of these ladies. As a rookie, I can only dream of playing like the veterans one day.

2 – LIKE POPCORN

In the vernacular of Rodney Dangerfield, substitute bus drivers don't get no respect. Some regular-route bus drivers are aware of this. They tell me that they won't tell their kids when there is going to be a substitute. That way the kids won't have time to make nefarious plans.

It's a fact that the kids act differently for the regular bus driver than for the substitute. I will ride with the regular bus driver to get familiar with the route before the day I will be substituting. The regular bus driver, who may have been driving for as many as twenty years, knows each of the kids by name. As she drives she will be keeping an eye on the kids in the rear-view mirror. As quick as a flash she will grab the intercom microphone, call a kid by name, and let him know what's going to happen if he does that again. For good measure she may add, "And don't give me that look!" This routine might happen several times on a morning or afternoon route. Does it work? Yes. On the routes where I've ridden with the regular driver there is a semblance of order and the noise is held to a dull roar.

When I drive that same route as a substitute it's like New York City during a blackout—there is looting and lawlessness. The bus driver has given the kids assigned seats. She knows which kids to keep separated and who should be sitting in the front near her. If a kid dares sit amiss the regular bus driver catches him or her quickly with a glance in the mirror. Sometimes she doesn't even need to use the intercom; she just gives the kid "the eye" via the mirror and the errant kid repents.

"Do we have to sit in assigned seats?" kids will ask as they board when they see they have a substitute.

"Yes." I say calmly. I can't let them know that I'm nervous. I am at a huge disadvantage. I have no idea where the kids are supposed to sit. Some of the kids have figured this out. They take advantage of my ignorance and sit next to the friend the regular driver has taken pains to separate them from. I know this only because other kids sometimes call them on it.

"Bus Driver! Billy isn't in his assigned seat!"

I catch glimpses of kids popping from one seat to another like popcorn. I see no rhyme or reason to it—it's just because they can. They can because I don't know their names. If I get on the intercom and yell, "Hey, you!" I have sixty-five kids staring up at me with eyes that say, "You talking to me?" Sometimes the popcorn kid will make the mistake of making eye-contact with me in the mirror while in the act of changing seats. I raise a questioning eyebrow. They sit still for about two intersections, then they pop again.

Not knowing any names I can't single out the epicenter of the deafening cacophony to apply some noise cancellation. On one particular afternoon route the noise went from cacophonous to insane. All the kids were yelling. Some of them were screaming. I don't mean screaming words; they were just screaming for the sheer joy of it.

Then there were those who pretended to try to help me. "BEEEE QUIIIIIETTTTTT!" they shouted at the top of their lungs. Then they grinned.

As a sub I have learned to hunker down and tell myself, "Just forty minutes and the bus will be silent again." On this day I couldn't take any more of it. I pulled the bus over onto the shoulder and stopped. This alone quieted the bus. The kids knew something was up. I unbuckled my seat belt, got up, and turned to face sixty-five pair of eyes.

I was very articulate. "Shut up!" I said. I went on. "I don't mind you talking and enjoying yourselves, but what's with the screaming?"

That was it. I beat Abraham Lincoln's Gettysburg Address for brevity if not in beauty. Most had looks on their faces that said, "Whoa, that was unusual for a sub." They were back up to a dull roar before we went a quarter-mile, but they did keep it just under insane.

When I dropped them off many said, "Thanks for the ride," or "See ya." I was the only traumatized one on the bus. Since then, that route has become one of my favorites to sub on.

There is another route that drops kids at different spots along ten miles of highway. The regular driver knows just where on this highway to stop. I don't. One tree or fence post looks like another to my inexperienced eye. Even after a familiarization ride with the regular, I can't make heads or tails out of the stops. As Blanche says in *A Streetcar Named Desire,* "I have come to depend upon the kindness of strangers." This translates into me asking the nearest student where the next stop is. In almost every case the students have been extremely helpful. They seem to take pride in getting me where I need to be. When they haven't been helpful, they've been playful: Several high school students are getting off at the next stop. I call back to them, "Right here?"

"No," call out five voices. "It's up there."

"Okay," I say, and continue to roll up the highway.

"NO," call out five different voices. "It's right here!"

I'm in a predicament. I have no idea how to tell which group of kids is telling the truth. I question them again and both sides are adamant. I make my decision and roll to the "farther" stop. There are yells of triumph and cries of anguish from the back of the bus. Five kids get up to leave the bus. The last one, a tall girl with long brown hair, speaks as she passes. "It was back there," she said. I'd been got.

Being a substitute bus driver is not easy. It's not so bad, either. For all the noise and being taken advantage of, I am meeting an awful lot of great kids Everywhere I go kids will wave at me. These kids don't just give me a quick wave; they wave enthusiastically with a big smile. Most of the time I don't recognize them, but I know they are from the bus. This always touches me. I'm only a substitute bus driver, but for some reason I matter to them. This makes the entire experience matter to me.

3 – ANXIETY OF HUGS

Driving a school bus involves anxiety. If you asked the average Joe on the street what he would be most anxious about when driving a school bus he would say, "Dealing with a busload of riotous kids." Yes, there is anxiety in that. But, wait, it gets worse.

What about driving a load of forty-five high schoolers on the freeway in rush hour? You need to change lanes to make the exit. If you miss the exit they will be late for their event. The kids in the back are teasing and laughing and oblivious to the semi-truck on your right, the mini-van on your left and the wave of brake lights rising up in front of you. It gets even worse.

Each year the safety supervisor shows us drivers a video during the yearly bus driver safety training. This year the video features a man who had been a bus driver for fifteen years. He is of a humble disposition—maybe even a little broken in spirit. We quickly learned why. During a moment of distraction, after unloading two little boys, he unknowingly ran over one of them. The boy died and the driver landed in jail. When the video ended one of our longtime bus drivers broke the silence saying, "I quit." Yes, there is anxiety involved in driving a school bus.

There are a lot of rules we are trained and retrained on aimed at keeping the kids safe. Most are involved with loading and unloading. We are taught to turn on our yellow flashers before we arrive to let following cars know we are stopping. The yellow flashers turn to red and our stop signs extend when we open the door. We position the bus well out in the road to help discourage traffic from passing. We stop before we reach the line of kids to make them come to us. They are supposed to wait for us to point to the door before the move toward the bus.

There are so many rules, but it doesn't take long to see why. When you approach a bus stop most of the kids are already in a huddle or a line waiting for you. Sometimes the group surges before the bus has stopped. Often kids who are late come running for the bus. They might be approaching from the rear or running across the street in front of you. Sometimes there is shoving going on; a child might be pushed out in front of the bus. I've seen Frisbees land in the road and a child will ignore the approaching forty foot bus to retrieve it.

After the kids load, you take the time to look in all your mirrors to make sure there are no kids standing beside the bus, or worse, crawling under the bus after something they dropped. You close the door and let the bus roll forward at dead idle so that you can stop more quickly just in case you suddenly see something you didn't see before. Doing these things isn't necessarily difficult. What is difficult is doing these things *consistently* day after day, week after week. You might be distracted by difficulties at home, a headache, or a student who is having a bad day. Keeping the safety focus is difficult for a human being.

I was unloading children at various stops along a busy highway. A car was following close behind my bus. I'm sure the driver was frustrated each time he saw the flashing, red, "STOP" sign extend. As I braked and stopped at the house with the cute, little, miniature horse out front my attention turned to a ten-wheel dump truck approaching from the other direction. I had turned my yellow flashers on before I stopped warning him of what I was going to do. If he was empty he would have no trouble stopping. He had a full load of gravel. I had a brother and sister who were getting off and who would be crossing the highway to their home. The speed of the dump truck and the look in the truck driver's eyes told me he wasn't going to be able to stop. His load was too heavy. His brakes were squealing, but the truck wasn't slowing. He was imagining what I was imagining—that kids would run across the road as he arrived. I was able to stop them before they got out, and the tragedy didn't happen.

Another day I stopped on a residential street to unload a boy. Two cars obeyed my red STOP sign and stayed behind me. In my rear-view mirror I saw the boy stand up in the back of the bus. He would work his way up the aisle and in a moment he would be off. I waited, but he never arrived at the front. I looked back to see what was happening. He was working his way toward the front, but was taking time to hug each person on the bus as he went. I was substituting on this route and wasn't familiar with the young man. Apparently he was mentally handicapped in a manner that made him very friendly. I watched the other students' reactions as he reached them. Some smiled and hugged back. Others just endured the love. I was aware of the drivers waiting behind the bus and imagined them slapping their steering wheels in impatience. I was tempted to yell at the boy to stop it and just get off. I checked in the mirror again and decided to keep my mouth shut. Seeing the boy's good will and the good nature of the kids being hugged, I didn't want to be the one to ruin it.

As he finally approached the front of the bus I looked at the twelve-year-old girl who had been showing me where the stops were and said, "Here comes your hug." She rolled her eyes as if to say "What we have to put up with on this bus." When the boy hugged her I saw her grin. He finally exited the bus and I was able to let the cars behind me go. I don't know how impatient the drivers of the cars actually felt, but I thought they could probably use a hug.

4 – THE LAST GIRL ON THE BUS

In the mornings the kids get on the bus sleepily. Very few of them will answer my chipper "Good morning." They sit at the back in the pre-winter dark like tombstones in a graveyard. In the afternoon these same kids bounce onto the bus full of vinegar and energy. Some of the more thoughtful kids will meet my eyes and say "hello," but most look past me to the seat and the company they want. The noise level rises so that I can't hear the chatter on the bus-to-bus radio. The constant movement I see in my rearview mirror reminds me of what I see when I look down on an ant pile.

It's ten miles to the small town where I am taking this load. One mile outside of town limits, I begin looking forward to the first stop where I can release some of the pressure that has built up inside the bus. It's better after the first stop, but it isn't until after the second stop that I actually feel relief. The kids driving most of the chaos are gone now. While I still see many faces looking back at me in the mirror the remaining kids have returned to their human state. I can see their afternoon plans passing behind their eyes as they await their stops.

Finally the last child climbs down the steps and turns up the street, backpack swinging on one shoulder. I raise the steering wheel, release my seatbelt, and begin to walk the bus to make sure a sleeping child hasn't missed his stop. I only walk halfway to the back when I stop. There is a girl sitting in the third to last seat next to the window. She lifts her eyes from the book she is reading and meets mine. Such a stillness had come over the bus when the "last" child got off that I

14

hadn't suspected that anyone else was still riding. I give an embarrassed laugh. "I didn't see you," I say.

This last girl on the bus lives at a dairy—another three miles out of town. Sometimes she is on the afternoon bus. Sometimes she isn't. The bus can legally hold 84 students. For these last miles she has it all to herself. I glance at her in the mirror as we roll up the highway. She's sitting higher in her seat now. Her complexion and hair are fair, mixing well with the sunlight that comes through her window. It is almost like camouflage. I can see how I missed her on the last stop. She stares out the window at the pastures and sagebrush. My daughter and this last girl on the bus have been friends for a long time. They both dance and dream. This girl talked her mom into getting her a mermaid costume. For an entire summer she wore her tail in their little fill-up-with-a-hose pool. Central Utah suddenly had mermaids. The world needs more dreamers like that.

Each time I chauffeur her in her private, yellow coach she is quiet. I always wonder what dreams fill her mind.

I pull into the dairy entrance, stop, and open the door. The cows are curious and stare. Their barnyard stinks.

"Have a good afternoon," I say.

She flashes a quick smile. "Bye," she returns.

She waves at some dairy employees as she begins her walk across the gravel yard to her home at the other end of the compound. She walks with the grace of a dancer. She carries her head with the lightness of a dreamer. She is on the cusp of adulthood. I sense her hopes for the future. I foresee the disappointments she will face. As I watch her, my hopes and dreams for my own daughters walk with her—this last girl on the bus.

5 – ONE COLD MORNING

Every school bus compound is filled with buses of varying ages. Buses built twenty years ago will be sitting next to buses fresh off the factory floor. Each of these buses is assigned a number. This seems a shame to me. Buses have personalities, so wouldn't it be more interesting if the buses had names? The middle school bus with all its unruly seventh and eighth graders could be The Beast. One of the buses that make the long run to Rocky Ridge would be Geronimo. The bus with the sweet little kindergarten kids might be Serenity. Bus names would make the daily runs more meaningful. I think Tennessee Williams understood this when he wrote *A Streetcar Named Desire*. But of course we are dealing with the public school system— "public" being the operative word. You mix creativity with "public" and you are going to have trouble. Someone is going to suggest we burn *Huckleberry Finn* for being racist, or destroy Michelangelo's David for being obscene. There is an older bus that I could see named Puff the Magic Dragon because of the exhaust trail if leaves behind. I imagine that name could be taken the wrong way. We play it safe and give our buses plain, inoffensive, efficient numbers.

In our district the bus numbers represent the model year. Thus, 970 is a 1997 model and 014 is the 2014 model. If two buses were purchased the same year you might have 011 and 011A. You might think that bus drivers would jump at the newest bus. They don't. They tend to stick with the bus they trust. The driver of 06 has been driving twenty-two years. With her seniority she could take the new bus when it comes in. But the new bus is unproven whereas 06 has never let her down badly enough to be fired. She forgoes the heated seat and exhaust brake to stick with her partner—06.

The other morning it was 22° below zero. This had taken us by surprise because the day before the temperature was in the 40's. In spite of engine block heaters and anti-gel additive in the diesel some of the buses wouldn't start. Pneumatic doors wouldn't open or close. One windshield defroster couldn't keep up with the moisture emitted by seventy breathing kids. The bus driver had to stop because she couldn't see.

I was called at the last moment by a driver whose bus wouldn't start. This was her backup bus. Her regular bus's transmission went out the day before and stranded her in the middle of town. I ran out to 001 and turned the key. It started, but it choked, gasped, and coughed for some time before dieseling properly. The cloud of half-burnt diesel that engulfed my house could have gotten me a citation from the EPA. When I finally put it in gear and gave it a little throttle the bus wouldn't move. I had already disengaged the park break so I didn't know what was wrong. I gave it a little more throttle; there was a crack as the wheels broke free of the ice bonding them to the ground and the bus started rolling. The heat pump was on, but it would be twenty minutes before it produced any heat. A frosty windshield and thick ground fog—the kind with a blue sky above—shrouded my way. I had to drive slowly.

It was so cold that kids who had been waiting on time at their stops had run back to their homes. I stopped at one rural home to see if the kids would come out. Sure enough the door opened and two faces peeked out. A brother and sister came running up their long driveway.

"Where were you? My hair froze solid!" the sister told me.

I apologized.

A couple of miles later two other boys came running out of their home when they saw me.

"We waited," they told me, apologetically, "but we went back home."

The other kids normally at that stop weren't there. I didn't blame them.

There was loads of chatter on the radio. Arrangements were being made for drivers to pick up another driver's kids.

"014, after dropping off your kids at the elementary can you go back to pick up 012's kids on the highway?"

"I'm at Bursten's Road. I think I'm closer," says 002.

Complaints about non-functioning doors were coming in. Suggestions were being given on how to defrost the windshield. Another driver whose route overlapped mine called to ask me where I was. She told me she would tell the frozen kids I was coming. I turned a corner and there was a large group huddled together. Their breath rose into the sky in a frosty cloud. There were several running vehicles sitting there with slightly warmer kids inside. I opened the door and the kids started filing in. Wouldn't you know it, they were smiling. At least the elementary students were. The teenagers—not so much.

"Cold, cold, cold," exclaimed one girl as she passed. She wasn't even three-feet tall yet. Her cheeks and nose were red. Her blue eyes peeked out from under a penguin hat. Fuzzy tassels ran down each side of her face.

My door still wasn't closing all the way. I asked a little fellow in the front seat if he would step down and push on it for me. He happily complied. The door shut and the stairway light went out.

"At each stop I have to push on the door, okay?" He felt important.

We came around the corner and I saw 008 sitting in front of the fire department. It was the bus that had broken down there the night before. The tow truck hadn't come to get it yet. All the windows were frosted over. It looked lonely and out of place. I could almost sense its sadness as all of the kids that would normally ride it passed by.

"Don't worry," I told it silently as I drove 001 out of town. "You'll get better and they'll be back."

6 - FACES LIKE MUSIC

Unlike teachers who spend hours, days, and weeks with the local youth population, school bus drivers only see the kids for a few seconds each day. Although the drive to and from school takes longer than that, we only actually see the kids when they are getting on or off the bus. My contact with each child each day may be short, but in those few seconds I get snapshots of the children's lives that, while not telling me much, do tell me something.

I took the junior high school run the other afternoon. When I opened the doors, a line of preteens and early-teens streamed in. Awkwardness and angst sloughed off of them like dust from Pigpen in *Charley Brown*. I had an unexpected flashback to my own junior high days, with all its memories of loneliness and confusion. The face of one boy stood out as he got on the bus—pimples, rough, raw. I saw this face again near the end of the route when I walked to the back of the bus to investigate a spitting incident. A girl reported that this boy had spit out the window. The airflow through the open windows caused the spit to fly back into the next window and onto the girl's face. I didn't look forward to confronting him. His face had a large amount of "I couldn't care less" written all over it. His "I couldn't care less" expression faded into nervousness as I approached. This gave me hope. We chatted for a moment. I helped him understand what happens when you spit out a window on a bus. He understood there would be greater consequences if he did it again. As I walked away it struck me that he really hadn't intended to be rude to the girl he accidentally spit on. He just didn't have a lot of common sense.

Early one Saturday morning the girls' volleyball team got on the bus. I said "Good morning" to one girl as she passed. She didn't respond—didn't even glance my way. I noticed she walked halfway back and took a seat some distance from the other girls. It may have been she wasn't a morning person. Maybe there was trouble at home or with the other girls. I couldn't tell. One of the other girls came up to the front of the bus to offer me a muffin. Somehow, within the horizon of her early morning ride, she saw the bus driver. I was touched.

I was dropping a load of elementary kids off at school. One third-grader was dressed in a colorful dress and leggings. As she stepped onto the sidewalk I called out, "That's a pretty dress." There were lots of kids filing out right behind her so I didn't think she would hear. She did. She looked over her shoulder and flashed a happy smile of pure sunshine that warmed me for a week. The last girl off the bus that day wore a blue blanket with a shark-head hood. It looked like her head was in the shark's mouth. It was cute. As she walked down the aisle I said, "Sharks are not allowed on the bus." She wasn't sure if I was seriously scolding her or not. Then I said, "I like your blanket." She stopped beside me, smiled, and gave a big, happy, sigh.

One day when I was a substitute driver I picked up eight kindergarteners. We drop kindergarteners off at their homes. I had never driven this route and didn't know where they lived. I asked them for help and they excitedly complied. There were no "drive to the highway and turn left" kind of instructions. Instead I had eight kids calling out, "Drive this way. Then turn that way!" I had to look in the mirror and try to decipher their finger pointing. One little boy adamantly indicated I should go down "this street." I did. Two other kids overrode his instructions telling me it was the street with the "rocks" on it. It took a moment, but then I realized they meant the gravel road by the edge of the subdivision. I knew where that was. As we approached a pasture with cows they told me to honk. "Our regular bus driver does," they said. My bus has an air horn. It sounds like a train when you pull the cord. I look for opportunities to use it. I gave it a yank. Eight voices yelled out in unison, "Hello, cows!" And they waved. Heading up the highway I saw three bored-looking horses in a dusty corral. I yanked the cord again and pretended I was a train. The five remaining kids yelled out, again in perfect unison, "Hello, horses." Once more they waved. I eventually got each child home and watched him or her run happily to the parent waiting in the doorway.

Some cars, not very many, still have radios that are tuned by a dial. If the dial is turned fast, voices and music quickly resolve and then disappear in fragments. A practiced ear can get a sense of what the fragment of sound was about. Being a bus driver is much like turning the radio dial. Instead of sounds, faces flash past giving a momentary glimpse into a child's day or life. It isn't much of a glimpse; it is just enough to make me care.

7 - THE LITTLE BUS THAT COULD

At 6:45 a.m. on a morning when the temperature was -20° F I received a call from the bus coordinator. Two of the three buses in our little town wouldn't start due to the cold. He asked me to see if my bus would start. If it would I was to pick up as many kids as would fit and take them to school. The school is located thirteen miles away in the neighboring community. Our town may be tiny, but there are a lot of children. The three regular buses are normally fairly full.

I dressed for the cold and ran out to my bus. Maybe I should explain, my bus is a special bus. It's designed to hold only eighteen students with room for a wheelchair in the back. I drive this bus from the school to our little community each night with five or six kids who stay late after school for tutoring or extracurricular activities. Compared to the big buses it looks like a baby bus. It's not nearly as tall and is far shorter.

It was cold. My door opened with a *crack*. My bus had an engine core warmer plugged in, but so did the other buses that wouldn't start. I turned the key. The bus belched thick, grey smoke, but then the diesel engine started to chug. That was a blessing on such a cold morning.

I got on the radio and told the supervisor the bus was running. I could hear the stress in his voice as he repeated his instructions to pick up as many students as I could fit. The bus I was replacing seated eighty-four kids. He had 150 kids to get to school from this community and not enough buses to get them there. It seemed to me that the eighteen kids I had seats for wasn't going to do much good.

The other bus that was running in town radioed and asked if I would go to the west side and pick up kids there. She was picking up two routes of kids herself. When I turned onto 4th South I saw a line of kids waiting at the first stop. They broke into laughter when they saw the baby bus. Their smiles were so big they almost cracked their frozen cheeks. The baby bus doesn't get the same respect as the big buses. The baby bus is the *Little Engine That Could* compared to the big diesel locomotives. When I pulled up beside them and opened the doors I heard one boy say incredulously, "No way!" He was wondering if he could survive the indignity of riding in such a bus.

More than three-quarters of my eighteen seats filled up on that first stop. Normally morning runs are quiet because all the kids are still half-asleep. The severe cold and the surprise appearance of the baby bus fully awakened the kids. They chattered and laughed loudly as we continued. A large number of kids awaited at the next stop. Like the first group they looked at the baby bus with wide eyes and grins.

"Three to a seat," I called as the new group started filing on. Three to a seat was asking a lot since all the kids wore bulky winter clothing and toted backpacks. I got up to help arrange kids. A mother, who had walked her student to the bus stop, stood outside saying nothing but giving me a look that said, "You really think you are going to get all those kids on that little bus?" I was thinking the same thing.

The seats ran out quickly. However, the baby bus had a large empty space in the back. Six seats had been removed to accommodate a wheelchair lift.

"Shall we stand in back?" asked some of the high school students. The sign in the front of the bus announced an occupancy limit of 32. That's how many could be seated if all the seats were available.

"Sure," I said. I didn't want to leave any of the kids at this stop waiting out in the -20° F cold for another bus that might not come for thirty minutes. Bigger kids gave their seats to the younger kids and squeezed shoulder to shoulder in the back. No one complained. They laughed at the fun and felt warmer standing close. One of the students counted heads. I had thirty-one on that little bus when I pulled away. The other bus that was running packed the children in, too. Somehow she was able to pick up all the remaining kids in town. They were like sardines in a can, but no one had to stand.

We radioed our supervisor and told him we had picked up all the kids. Somehow a bus and a half had squeezed in three busloads of kids. "It's kind of like the miracle of the loaves and fishes," said the supervisor. I could hear the relief in his voice.

If anyone watched the endless line of kids get out of my little bus they might have thought of clowns getting out of a tiny car at the circus—the doors of the little bus opened and the line of kids that got out never seemed to end. I had a difficult time keeping the grade-schoolers in their seats on the way to the elementary school. They wanted to stand in the back. They arrived at school late, but they arrived alert and excited. All the buses were running by afternoon, so the excitement was over.

I attended the town Christmas celebration that night. Several elementary students waved at me excitedly as I got in the chili line. "Hi, Tory!" they called. They had been on the bus that morning. After getting my chili and roll I found a seat near a covey of middle-school girls. Middle schoolers generally won't make eye contact with their bus driver, let alone talk to them. That's why the girl had to speak twice before I realized she was speaking to me.

"That was crazy this morning," she said with a smile.

"Yes, it was," I answered.

The girl next to her chimed in, "I was, like, 'That little bus isn't going to stop for us.' When it did I was, like, 'No way!'"

"Everyone at school was talking about it all day," added the first girl. "It was so much fun."

"I don't think it would be so fun a second time," I said.

They laughed; they weren't so sure.

8 - GETTING MY BOSSY ON

I'm glad I started driving bus as a substitute driver. It gave me valuable experience and an important reference point. Having said that, I need to make it clear that I don't ever want to be a substitute bus driver again. Substituting is tough. You don't know the routes; you don't know who's supposed to be on the bus and who isn't; and hardest of all, you don't know the kids' names. I've learned that not knowing the kids' names is like riding a horse without a bridle—you don't have a lot of control.

I started my own route half-way through the school year. I was excited that finally I would have enough repetition to learn the kids' names. Looking in my rearview mirror at the seventy-five kids gave me second thoughts. How could I ever remember all their names? Ironically it took the kids forever to realize I was their permanent driver.

"Where's our bus driver?"

"I'm your bus driver now."

"Oh. So when is our bus driver going to be back?"

I started to get to know the kids who ventured to the seats up front. They were curious about me. I learned a little from them.

"You're nicer than our last bus driver," they told me. "You don't yell as much."

Another student mentioned that I got around the route much faster than the old bus driver.

"She stopped a lot to yell and make kids sit down."

These sound like compliments, yet I wasn't so sure.

"I think I should be stricter," I said. I was a rookie bus driver, but something told me I was right.

"No! No!" they yelled.

In truth I didn't want to be like the other bus drivers. I had ridden with several while being trained. They did a lot of serious intercom enforcing.

Brayden, you do that again and you'll be having a conference with the principal.

Lisa, pipe down! And don't give me that look!

During training I sat in the front passenger seat and couldn't see in the mirror. I didn't see what it was the Brayden was doing or the look Lisa gave the driver. I've seen the look plenty since then—slitted eyes and narrowed lips.

During the training rides it wasn't the kids, but the veteran bus drivers that scared me. I wondered if I was going to have to be like them and yell a lot. I wondered if I could be like them even if I wanted to.

The bus driver I replaced drove for fifteen years and was a very fine bus driver. I rode with her a couple of times to learn the bus and the route and I did notice how quickly she got on the intercom to call kids out. She wanted kids in their seats facing forward and she wanted a low noise level. It took a lot of effort, and noise, on her part every day to make this happen.

When I started driving the route I was much more laid back. Even though I didn't want to be a bus driver who did a lot of yelling, my "laidback-ness" wasn't so much a conscious choice as it was I didn't know what I was doing. I didn't know the kids' names so it was, "You! You in the back. Sit down." The two kids standing and facing backward ignored me while the two kids sitting properly in the seat across the aisle looked at me and pantomimed, "Who? Us?"

My line in the sand for the students' behavior was a wavy one. I made sure they didn't stand in the aisles, but other than that neither they, nor I, knew the boundaries. I was known as the nice bus driver, but I had an uneasy feeling that wasn't necessarily a good thing.

In the afternoons my kids were happy, but they were noisy and barely under control.. They came out of school all wound up. Expecting them to sit quietly on a bus was the same as expecting a cat to fetch a stick. To be fair there was nothing scandalous going on. Some of the kids would make a game of hopping from seat to seat when they thought I wasn't looking. Other kids had a habit of standing up to talk to someone in another seat. These things were safety hazards and annoying, not actually evil. As I slowly learned their names I called them on the behavior. They would stop for a few minutes, and then start again. The fact that I had to ask them again and again gave me the sense that I wasn't in control.

I thought my problem was that I had no authority to punish the kids for their behavior. I'm not allowed to throw kids off the bus or tell them they can't ride. A bus driver wants to be careful about touching a kid for any reason. How was I supposed to get the kids to take me seriously if I couldn't effectively enforce the rules? It seemed like a no-win situation and I was feeling pretty low.

One day, after the morning route, I talked with a bus driver who had been driving eighteen years. She was a natural disciplinarian and ran a pretty tight ship. In vague terms I described the troubles I was having on my bus. She told me one thing that made a difference for her was keeping the kids from being in the aisle. She drew a firm line there. It wasn't much to go on, but it was something.

The next morning a couple of high school boys in the back were leaning across the aisle to look at an iPad someone held in the other seat. I asked them to get out of the aisle. They did. A minute later they were in the aisle again. I repeated my request and once more they moved back. When they leaned across the third time I gathered all my courage and told them to come to the front. High school kids do not like to sit in the front with the grade school kids. It's humiliating. To my relief they complied. They were embarrassed and unhappy about it, but they came. The bus grew quiet as they walked up the aisle. These two brothers were good kids; both were Eagle Scouts. If they were in trouble then anyone could get in trouble. They sat down near me and I explained the safety issue involved with leaning out in the aisle. They were grumpy, but they listened. I've had very little trouble with them since.

I was a different bus driver when I got off the bus that morning. It wasn't that keeping kids from leaning into the aisles is the answer to controlling a load of kids; it was the confidence I gained when I called those two brothers on the rule. No longer did I feel I had no control over my kids. I learned then, and in several experiences since, that the kids aren't "bad" and that they will listen to me. I have to give a nod to their parents for this, but the kids have a respect for authority. I just had to start believing in my authority first.

My daily bus experience is still an adventure. I have to call out "stay put" or "sit down" at least once each run—usually more. It's not uncommon that I have to ask someone to come sit up front to remove them from a troublesome situation. I almost turned in a middle school girl the other day for repeatedly standing to talk to someone behind her. On the third call, when I got stern, she rolled her eyes and said something I'm glad I didn't catch. She stayed put after that third call, and since that day I haven't had to ask her to sit down again.

Keeping my kids under a reasonable level of control is a constant effort, but I no longer have my fear of not being in control. Sometimes when I call a kid on unacceptable behavior I will see a look that says, "I can't believe I put up with this." But they do put up with it just as I put up with them. They are pretty good kids.

In learning how to get my bossy on I've probably lost my "nicest bus driver" status. Even so, I still love seeing my kids each day and most seem happy enough to see me. We just respect each other a little more now.

9 - THAT TRUCK DRIVER MYSTIQUE

Not once in all my years did driving a school bus cross my mind. Not when I was in elementary school (I was going to be a fighter pilot). Not when I was in high school (I was going to be an astronomer). Not when I was getting a master's degree in college (I was going to be a writer). All I knew about being a school bus driver I learned from *The Simpsons*. Perhaps you remember the bus driver: long-haired, acid-rock-listening, slightly-stoned-sounding Otto Mann? It wasn't until I reached a slightly more desperate time in my life when an acquaintance and school bus driver made me aware of an upcoming opening on the local school bus driving force that I looked into a career change.

I still remember the first time I climbed into the driver's seat of the bus, popped the parking break, and eased out of the bus compound onto the public streets. In my youth I had driven a ten-wheel truck during the potato harvest in Idaho. While in college I had driven a dump truck and a garbage truck. I had never driven something forty feet long where the front wheels were six feet behind me. It was exciting. What made it so exciting was that driving the bus felt like I was driving a truck—you know, the big eighteen-wheeler kind of truck. Every man has thought at least once of getting behind the wheel of one of those and rumbling down the freeway. My bus had air brakes that hissed and squelched. It had clearance lights along with many other exterior lights that lit it up like a circus. Best of all was the air horn. Yes, I pulled the cord a few times just for the fun of it.

On my first highway drive I passed a semi going the other way. The truck driver and I looked at each other in the eye. I excitedly commented to my trainer, "I'm sitting as high as a truck driver!" She just smiled.

Even though my bus had everything a semi had, it was still just a school bus. I might sit as high, have as many lights, and have an air-horn, but I'm not driving a long-haul truck. There is a difference seeing a bright yellow, flat-faced school bus coming down your street and seeing a semi with its long trailer rolling slowly past.

It hadn't occurred to me that I had passed the same test that truck drivers pass. The only difference was that I took the passenger angle of the test while they took the trailer angle. I had a Class C commercial driver license. Us professionals call that a CDL. I had no reason to feel inferior to the truck driver because he carries frozen potatoes and I carry seventy children. Cargo is cargo and the kids are worth a lot more.

It wasn't until I was driving the high school choir on a special event trip that I felt validated as a professional driver. The freeway was busy. Cars and trucks weaved in and out as they sparred for position. Buses aren't particularly fast, but on a hill I passed a semi that, under a full load, struggled a little. I signaled that I was going to pull back in front of him. In my rear-view mirror I saw him blink his lights at me to let me know that I was clear. What a thrill. I had seen truck drivers do that for each other throughout my years as a private driver. Now one had done it for me. He had shown me a professional courtesy. I sat a little higher in my seat. It wasn't too many more miles down the road when I passed another semi. I looked over as I passed. The truck driver gave me the two-fingered salute that starts at the brow and swings forward. It was done casually like, "We professional drivers understand each other." My spine tingled at the validation. He had shown me the respect of an equal. Now I sat completely straight in my air-cushioned seat. I held my head high and proud.

A month later I was assigned to drive the girls' basketball team and their coaches to a game in Coalville, UT. To get there I had to drive 101 miles and navigate the 7,120-foot Parley's Summit. In the city, where the trip began, the sky was overcast and the roads were dry. By the time we reached Salt Lake City the skies had gone from gray to black. Hail-like snow started hammering against the bus.

Behind me, I saw drowsy heads pop up to see what was going on. I'm sure they wished they had stayed asleep because it only got worse. By the time I turned onto the belt-route it was snowing heavily. The roads were covered.

Oh, great, I thought. My anxiety level was rising.

By the time I reached Parley's Canyon we were in an all-out blizzard. Snow wasn't falling; it was attacking. The wind drove it angrily across the road. It would swirl and rise back up into the sky against the current before falling suddenly again. I saw what looked like a hundred trucks pulled over putting on chains.

I slowed down to a crawl and wondered if I should drive on. The bus didn't have chains. Stopping basically meant turning around and going home. What about the game? It seemed important to get to our destination and I believed if I just drove slowly we could do so safely. I decided to go forward.

Still, I had moments of doubt. I contemplated how I came to find myself responsible for a bus full of kids on a mountain road in an angry January blizzard. I could feel the weight of their lives on my shoulders. I wondered if any of my passengers were scared. I know I was. The answer came when one of the coaches made his way up to the seat behind me. Leaning around the side he asked, as casually as he could,

"So this is your bus?"

"Yes."

"You drive it every day?"

"Every day."

"Okay," he said. He returned to his seat.

Translated, he was asking "How experienced are you and how scared should I be?" My answers were as vague as his questions, but he seemed satisfied.

The drive was slow.

"What time does the game start?" I asked a coach.

"They won't start without us," he deadpanned.

The girls were quiet in the back. The windshield wipers groaned on every other stroke. The defrosters howled and the two driver's fans were turned toward the windshield to help. We passed several

31

cars that had pulled off to the side to wait out the storm. The drivers looked up at me with frightened, questioning eyes as we passed. The storm didn't let up until we reached Coalville.

After I dropped the team off at the high school, a sense of euphoria came over me. It was the same feeling I felt after navigating a raft through Haystack Rapids on the Middle Fork of the Salmon River. The chaos and danger was behind us. I had driven safely and in control the entire way. I was proud of myself as a professional driver. The safe arrival also made me feel humble. I didn't want to drive back through that storm. Thankfully, I didn't have to. The storm had passed south by the time we returned.

It was some weeks later when I was driving the girls' basketball team to another game. We had to drive through an even narrower, more winding canyon to get to this one. Fortunately, the skies and roads remained clear. On the way home we stopped to eat. When the girls returned there was a lot of chatter and laughter as the girls filed past me. Suddenly one of the girls stopped. She put her fingers on my shoulder to get my attention.

"I just wanted to say thank you for driving so safely through that blizzard a few weeks ago. I've never been as scared." Then she went on to her seat.

I don't know who she was. It was dark so I couldn't see her face. Can teenagers be so thoughtful and kind? This girl certainly was. A school bus may not be a truck, but the kids we haul and the pleasant surprises they bring are worth it.

10 - THE COLORS OF A SCHOOL BUS

School buses may be bright yellow, but inside they are far more colorful.

It's 6:40 am. I pull up to the locked, west gate at the bus compound and get out to open it. Korleen is already in there with her bus started. She came in the east gate. She's checking her coolant as I saunter unenthusiastically to my bus. As I pass her I ask, "Haven't we done this before?"

"Seems like it," she says.

She's been "doing this" for fifteen years. It's only my second. I'm enjoying it, but I can't imagine being here in fifteen years.

At some point during the morning route I brake to a stop and hear a rattling behind me. I look down to see a herd of Peanut M&Ms stampeding to the front—green, yellow, and brown. A blue one brings up the rear.

Florence, a third grader, makes me nervous by getting out of her seat and bringing me up paper snowflakes. She does this twice. She's so sweet (usually) that it's hard to ask her to stay in her seat. I know that after the run, when I walk my bus to check for sleeping children, I'm probably going to find a pile of white snowflake makings six inches deep on the floor where Florence was sitting. That's the price of having an arts-and-crafter on board. I'm going to have to clean that up later.

In the afternoon I see little Leonardo sleeping in the front passenger seat. He's a wisp of a kindergartener who speaks English with a strong Spanish accent. A mop of fine, black hair sticks up from his head and , when he's awake, he looks at me with soft, black eyes. Right now he's leaning into the corner of the seat and bus wall. When I brake his upper body slides forward until his head hits the soft, padded wall in front of the steps. He doesn't wake. When I accelerate after the light turns green his upper body slides back into the corner. He doesn't feel a thing. When his brother wakes him at the dairy he doesn't know where he is. In the aisle he turns toward the back of the bus instead of the door. When we get him straightened out I make sure he grips both handrails before he descends the steps.

The next morning I notice a car is following me on one of the narrow back roads where there is little traffic. Its dirty, yellow headlights follow me around each corner. The Partons' porch light is off meaning the kids won't be riding today, so I don't stop. It's another two miles to my next stop. As the usual kids get on there I notice they are straining their necks looking behind the bus.

"Someone else is coming," Maryn tells me.

This is unusual. It turns out to be Arthur. He usually gets on a couple of stops back, but missed the bus this morning. His mother was chasing the bus.

That afternoon Arthur sits up front and tells me, "You made my mom swear this morning." He blushed a little when he told me this. His mother is a religious woman who normally frowns upon profanity.

"Oh?" I say. Angry parents are a bus driver's nemesis. I want to know more.

"When you didn't stop at the Andersons'," he explained. I told him I would have stopped if I had known who it was.

Eighteen kids get on at Churchyard Station. As they pass me I hear several kids going on about Kara farting. When kindergartener Kara gets on she stands very close to me. Whispering confidentially in my ear she says, "The kids all say I farted, but really I just stepped in dog poop." We both looked down at her shoes and then at each other. She shrugs and walks up the aisle.

Near the end of the morning route we stop at a house in the north fields. The sixth grade girl comes out in her striped rainbow socks with toes. In one hand she carries her tall boots which lace most of the way up to her knees. In the other she carries her books and a pop tart. She walks gingerly across the gravel and climbs the steps. I see her lacing her boots up in the aisle most of rest of the way to school.

A second grader is sitting in the front passenger seat because she feels like talking to me today. She wants to play Truth-or Dare. Truth-or-Dare is difficult to play while driving a bus, so I decline. In her innocent way she persists until I agree to give it a try. I choose "truth" on my turns because it's more practical. With a giggle she asks me if I have a girlfriend.

"Yes!" I say proudly and tell her my wife's name.

On another turn she asks me, with another giggle, if I have kissed my girlfriend.

"You bet," I tell her. She knows I am talking about my wife, which pleases her.

She chooses truth on her turn. I ask her, "When was the last time you told your dad you loved him?" She thinks for a moment. She mumbles her answer. I listen hard and make out that it has been a while. "Oh," I say, "I'm sure he deserves to hear that more often from you." She looks at me and smiles embarrassedly, "He's in jail," she says. I hadn't expected that. Those three words changed me a little bit.

Color is a wonderful thing—bright colors as well as the darker ones. Joseph has his coat of many colors. Michelangelo has his painter's palette. I have my school bus.

11 - A SCOLDING FROM SOMEONE
WHO LOVES YOU

I wake up to five inches of snow with more falling. It's just about six a.m. when I pull out of my driveway into the unplowed street. Sometimes I feel sorry for myself having to get up at five a.m to go to work. It feels like I am the only one leaving so early. The freshly fallen snow tells me a story that takes away some of my self-pity. On my way out of the small town where I live I see tire tracks coming into the road from four other driveways. They all left before me.

My Cummings diesel engine growls from behind as I pull out of the bus compound at 6:50. The houses across the street are still dark in sleep. I wonder if they are accustomed to my morning routine. Perhaps they use the sound of my engine and the flash of my headlights across their bedroom windows as an alarm clock.

I pick up my first stop of fifteen kids at the edge of town. Everything from kindergarteners to high school seniors get on. As usual, a kindergartener trips on the second step.

"Watch yourself," I say.

It's so routine that generally there's no response. The child catches himself and files silently past me with the rest into the dark seats beyond.

"Merry Christmas," I say to a tall high school boy as he climbs in. I'm surprised when he actually gives me a grin.

In just two blocks I reach the train tracks. On go the emergency flashers. I open my window, pop the parking brake, and open the door. I press the noise canceller and all the blowers on the bus turn off. The morning murmurings of the kids die with the blowers. I like to think they are helping me listen for trains, but I think they are only embarrassed to have their voices heard in the sudden silence. When I let go of the button the blowers kick back on and the murmurings begin again.

Once I enter the country I enter a world of black and white. It is black above and white below. The snow is falling heavily, but it isn't an angry storm. It's more of a scolding from someone who loves you. The narrow road is nowhere to be seen. The fallen snow is level from the field on the right to the field on the left. There are fences on both sides of the hidden road. I place the bus right in the middle and drive on faith. At the next house three of the four brothers and sisters are wearing Davy Crockett style raccoon hats. Furry tails trail down their necks and disappear behind their coat collars.

"Tory! Tory!"

I have just released the park break and we are beginning to roll when the little girl with the raccoon hat calls me from two seats back. She asks me if I like raccoon hats. I tell her I used to watch the Davy Crockett show on TV when I was a kid. She moves to the seat behind mine and tries to put her hat on me.

"Your head is too big," she says.

She tells me about her mom "petting" her dad's hair during morning prayer. "He said, 'I don't even have my Crockett hat on.'"

I drive down Airport Road, watching the big flakes of snow arc into the oversized windshield. I feel a childish gratification at making the first tracks on this road. Now, telephone poles on each side of the road give me my bearings. As two poles pass by, two more appear up ahead standing solid against the moving snow. Eventually I see the lights of the home that is my next stop. I squint and see three shadows moving up the driveway toward the road. Clusters of flakes lie on their hair like lace when they board. I see the wonder of the unexpected snow in their eyes as they pass me. I drive five miles to pick up one elementary girl. She walks slowly down her driveway and across the road—much more slowly than usual. She seems to be floating with the falling flakes. Her mind is elsewhere as she boards.

After dropping off the high schoolers I make my last elementary pickup in front of a church. One of the kids tells me that three of the others still haven't picked up "their rocks," which they threw in the church parking lot the day before. They had ignored my instructions to pick them when I dropped them off the night before. The rocks are big and create mounds of snow in the road. I call them up to the front and tell them to go put their rocks back. They obey without even a roll of the eyes. Three other boys ask if they can help. It's a chance to stretch their legs and get out in the snow. In thirty seconds they have the landscaping rocks back where they belong and we are driving to their school.

The snow makes us late arriving at the school. Four girls from the back of the bus take their time getting off. As the other kids make their way toward the school doors these girls stop to play. They don't seem to be aware that they are late. One girl puts snow in her mouth. The second girl kicks snow at the others. The third girl, the one with the brown eyes and freckles, tries to escape the snowball aimed at her neck by the fourth girl. She is laughing and waves to me as the bus doors close. Today there will be atrocities and horrors committed around the world, I know. But the beauty of this morning will be every bit as real and even more lasting.

12 - EDDY

At 5:00 am, when my alarm goes off, the faces of my bus children are already in my mind's eye. This is ironic since I only see many of these students' faces for mere moments each day. When they get on the bus I look directly into their faces. When they get off the bus I see their faces as a reflection in the mirror. Each face is just one piece of the puzzle of who they are. Over the course of the school year other pieces of the puzzle come into focus.

There is one child, I'll call him Eddy, who has caught my eye. He is one of a group of about twenty kids who get on at the Church stop and get off at the next stop, the elementary school. I have no assigned seats for them since they are on for less than ten minutes. They just clamber to the back of the bus.

Eddy, a second grader, got my attention by misbehaving. Mind you, most of the kids in the back are loud and boisterous, but Eddy tops them all. I am never surprised to see Eddy climbing over the seats or hanging out the window. What bothers me most is his telling other kids "**** you" and flipping them off. He only does this when he's mad, but he gets mad easily. I've seen him get off the bus after I've asked him to quit climbing over the seats and flip me off while shouting his favorite phrase.

Before you picture an ugly bully of a kid let me tell you that he the cutest little second grader you will ever see. He has dark hair, dark eyes, and a warm smile. Still, I felt compelled to turn him in to the principal when his imperative sentences (**** you) got out of hand.

The principal already knew him well. He said he would call him in and talk to him although he was already on detention.

It wasn't long before Eddy's language was making some of the older kids mad at him, so I turned him into the principal again. The principal, who really seems to love his kids, scratched his head. He told me he had talked to Eddy and his mom. His mom doesn't have a car. Throwing him off the bus would be throwing him out of school. I saw the problem. Eddy needs school. I didn't want to get in the way of his chance for progress if there was another way.

I moved Eddy and his big brother Shawn to the front of the bus. I didn't think for a moment that Eddy would quit using his language just because he was up by me, but it would limit who heard him. To my surprise Eddy and Shawn seemed happy to be in front. While sitting in the back they often had verbal altercations with the kids. Now, sitting up front, Shawn talked to me. He would tell me stories about the cars he is going to own when he grows up.

Eddy was quiet, but when he spoke I heard the sweet, high voice of a typical second grader. I didn't get to know him well, but I started seeing the little boy that he was. He liked to show me his Hot Wheels cars. When I showed interest he would shoot me his winning smile. Surprisingly, I never heard him swear once during the few weeks he was up front.

It wasn't all smooth sailing, though. Shawn would bully Eddy when Eddy didn't do what he wanted. They physically fought a couple of times. Usually it was only heated wrestling, but once I saw them exchange punches. Eddy won when he bit Shawn on the hand. Shawn, who is much bigger than Eddy, complained that Eddie was acting like a first grader.

The other day Eddy's teacher followed Eddy onto the bus after school. She sat with him in the front seat while the other kids boarded. She had a quiet, but earnest, chat with him while he sat with an angry pout on his face. As she left she said, "I'm sorry. Anything could happen. Anything!" She sounded at wit's end. I wasn't really sure what she was talking about, but I could guess that she was dealing with his classroom behavior. From what I had seen on the bus I could imagine her frustration.

The next day Shawn got on the bus and told me that Eddy wouldn't be getting on.

"They threw him out of school. He was kicking chairs over and flipping everyone off."

I learned Eddy had to complete an anger management class before they will let him back in school. I feel bad for the teacher. I feel bad for Eddy. I feel relieved that a potential problem is off the bus. I feel bad for feeling that relief.

13 - THIRTY MILES

Our city is a city of about five thousand people. The amount of space that the community covers would hold 100,000 or more in a bigger city. Even though the community is small and has lots of open space there are still people who feel crowded within the city limits. These people live west of town among the farmers' wheat, corn, and hay fields. When asked where they live these people will respond, "The West Fields." Even though there appear to be few houses scattered about in the fields, there are a surprising number of children who live there. My bus route is called the West Fields route. It covers thirty miles.

Every bus route has its nuances. In the morning mine starts with a girl standing by herself in the dark. In the winter she is typically standing on top of a pile of snow pushed there by the plows. I teased her once about being queen of the hill. She's a middle-schooler. Middle schoolers don't often talk to their bus driver, but this girl is friendly. When I called her Queen of the Hill, she stopped and considered it. She smiled and said, "Yes, I am." One morning she paused by my seat to show me pictures of the moon she had taken on her school iPad. The moon was full that morning and was setting in the West. "Cool," I said. Then I watched as she made her way down the narrow aisle to the last seat on the driver's side, her skinny form a silhouette against the back window.

The roads are narrow out in the west fields. They make odd, unexpected turns as they adjust for property lines. On one intersection the front end of my bus swings out over a ditch on the far side of the road while my rear duals clip the corner of another ditch on the near side. Not too much later the road takes a sharp ninety degree turn to the right. Eighty feet later it turns back ninety degrees to the left. Sometimes I will meet a farmer's truck hauling hay there. One of us has to wait for the other to negotiate the turns. There is always a friendly wave. After picking up the kids on the south end of the road I drive to a lonely intersection, do a three point turn, and go back the way I came. This is the only practical way to get to the other kids on the north end of the road.

There are three stops where a house sits off the narrow road far down an even narrower lane. The kids at these houses have to be brought up to the road to catch the bus. Some mornings they are late. As I approach the corner I will see headlights swing out from the driveway and then a plume of dust as the car speeds up the lane hoping that I don't pass by. I turn on my yellow flashers to let them know I see them.

There is a dairy on my route up on the hillside to the west of the valley. Several houses were built there for the families who work at the dairy. The houses sit above the dairy on a dirt road about a quarter mile away. When I pull into the dairy I make a U-turn by the red barn and position the bus so I can see the houses up on the hill. Sometimes a family is late and has to rush the kids down to the bus. If I see tail lights in the driveway I will wait for them. Sometimes I will see small shadowy shapes running to the car. I can almost hear the harried mother yelling at the kids to hurry. If they miss me at this stop it's six miles to catch me at the next stop.

After the dairy I drive down the highway back into the valley. After three miles I turn left onto Airport Road. There are cow pastures on the right and further down the road on the left sits the quiet, little airport with its lone green and white light rotating atop a striped pole. One day we passed three bald eagles sitting out in a field. Another day a red fox with its bushy tail ran across the road in front of us. There is only one house on that three-mile stretch of road and I don't stop there. I only take this road so that I can turn right where it T's off, go down a field length, and then turn back the way I came onto another road. It's the only way to get to another line of houses on the way back to town.

One morning four kids came running out of one of those homes. It was icy with a skiff of new snow. Three of the four kids slipped and landed in a pile in the middle of the road. After they got up one of them slipped and fell again. They were embarrassed, but okay.

Two little seven-year-old girls sit on the seat right behind me. They are cute as buttons. Both have a lot of energy. At the high school one of these girls hopped over to the seat by the door and touched each student on the head as they stepped down the stairs. Most ignored her. A few gave her the evil eye. She didn't seem to mind. Later I was driving along when I heard "Bus driver! Bus Driver!" in my left ear. One of these girls had climbed over the partition and stuck her head between my seat and the window to talk to me. Her face was so close to mine I could feel her breath on my cheek. A little disconcerted I told her to get back to her seat.

Some of the kids are on the bus for over an hour. Twice now a third-grade girl has called to me, "Could you hurry? My little brother has to poop." I can only hurry so fast while keeping it safe, but I do hurry.

My bus is new, with the padded, high-back seats. The seats are a safety feature. The problem is the kids can't see over them so they stand up or hang out into the aisles so they can talk with the other kids. It's a constant battle for me to keep the kids down in their seats for the duration of the ride. One day I noticed a middle-school girl leaning across the aisle to show a friend something on her phone. Using the intercom I called her back to her seat. Our eyes met through the rear-view mirror. The look on her face told me very clearly that she couldn't believe she had to put up with this.

My last stop in the mornings is in town. There are about fifteen kids who get on at the church parking lot. Some of the kids will still be walking to the stop when I turn the corner. When they see me they break into a run. Sometimes I will honk the air horn for their pleasure and mine and to hurry them along. The other kids are sliding on the ice in the parking lot or playing with bouncy balls. One cold morning they told me excitedly that they had been trying to build a fire to stay warm. I looked where they had been huddled together on the sidewalk. There were no signs of a failed fire. It made me wonder, though.

Every day those thirty miles are an adventure. Some days the bus feels happy. Other days it's ornery; or maybe that's just me. Each child is an ingredient, but even though the ingredients stay the same, the recipe never produces the same results on any given day. There is only one thing that is the same every day—the quiet after the last child has stepped off the bus. That quiet is a relief akin to taking off your shoes after a long day. But at least the day was filled with surprises.

14 - EVERY STOP HAS ITS OWN FLAVOR

My bus route is like an ice cream shop. E ach stop is a different tub with its own flavor.

My second stop, right at 7:00 am, is difficult to classify. At first I only see three or four kids waiting by the curb as I approach. When I stop several others will leap out of parents' cars where they have been waiting because it is cold outside. Still others come running out the front doors of their homes as I apply the brake. Eventually ten to fifteen will get on the bus.

The kids at this stop are neighbors, but not necessarily friends. Some will sit up front to talk with me. One girl always makes a point of giving me a cheery "good morning." Most of the others don't give me much more than a glance before making their way back into the dark of the bus. There was a time when kids from two different families were feuding. This led to some bus drama. There were tears and yelling as a close friendship broke apart. Another time someone from this stop complained to their mother that the bus was cold in the morning. The mother called the district. The district called my boss. My boss talked to me. The bus heater doesn't warm the bus until I am twenty minutes into the route. No one seems to care that the complaining kids don't wear coats even when it's below freezing outside. This stop is complicated. It's like an ice cream cone with four scoops of different flavors.

At the fourth stop I pick up a family of four kids. The high schooler and sixth grader never say much, but the second and first grader are always lively. They, Danny and Glory, will stop at my seat to point out the cat crossing the road or the foxes over in the field. They will point out their hideout they are making out of a piece of fencing and a railroad tie. Sometimes their dog Loki is at the stop with them. I've seen Glory dancing with the dog as I've pulled up. I've seen Danny feeding weeds to Hercules, their miniature horse. Once after I dropped this family off I went up to the cross roads where I made a 180 degree turn and came back down their road like I always do. Glory was up on the landscaping rock waving at me with both arms. She'd never done that before. I waved happily back and went on my way. It wasn't until three miles down the road that someone discovered Danny asleep on his seat. Glory was trying to let me know Danny hadn't gotten off. He had to ride another half hour before I could get him home. I radioed the office who called his home to let them know. The fourth stop is always entertaining. I like to think of it as Cherry Garcia.

Then there is the dairy. It is far out of town up on a hill. I stop the bus near the dairy barn. The kids live in a row of houses a half-mile further up the hill. The dairy is family owned and operated and the kids are all cousins. I can easily tell which kids are siblings because they look so much alike. Some of the kids are always waiting inside the milking barn where it is warm and come running out when I pull up. Another group of kids usually wait in a white pickup with their dad. A third group of kids may or may not catch the bus at this stop. They want to catch it, but often they are late and miss the bus. I will sometimes find them waiting at my eighteenth stop with my Churchyard kids. Their mom had to drive them eight miles to get them there. When they don't miss the bus it is usually because I see tail lights pulling out of a driveway far up the hill and decide to wait for them. I'll watch as the headlights guide a speeding vehicle down the dirt road. A van will skid to a stop near the bus, the doors open, and the kids spill out. They will be smiling as they get on the bus and more than one will thank me for waiting.

Just the other day at the dairy an eighth grader got on. He had been waiting in the barn with some other kids. At my seat he leaned down to look out the window and said, "My sister is coming." I looked up the hill to see a small figure running full speed down the gravel road. She is a first grader and very diminutive. I don't think she comes up to my waist. She ran like the wind through the dim, pre-dawn light to the bus steps. She climbed up breathing hard and smiling. I complimented her on her swiftness. She was proud. I shut the doors to go, but glanced once more up the hill. I saw a set of car lights swinging onto the gravel road from a driveway. Here came someone else. They were very late, but I didn't want to make them chase the bus for eight miles, so I waited. The car skidded to a stop beside the bus. I couldn't see who it was because the windshield was frosted over. The door opened and, remember the little girl who just ran the half-mile in record time? This was her second-grade sister. A brother and two sisters all arriving at the same stop at different times and in different manners? This stop never gets old. It reminds me of Vanilla Fudge Swirl.

I've already dropped the high schoolers and middle schoolers when I arrive at my eighteenth stop at the church parking lot. It usually looks like they are having a party. The fifteen kids are scattered all over the parking lot. Some are playing tag. A few are exploring the landscaping rocks. Four or five are trying to climb the young maple trees. When they see me turn the corner they come running from all directions and form a line next to their bags which they had carefully placed by the curb previously. One set of three brothers sometimes leaves their home late and are still a block away from the stop when they see me. They start running down the sidewalk ahead of me and turn it into a race. I honk my air horn to encourage them. The kids file onto the bus with noses and cheeks red from the cold. Some days they are smiling and excited for another day of school. Other days they tell on each other. I hear about who was mean to whom; who said swear words; and who was bold enough to "but" (but in line). The little kindergartener with the buzzed head climbs up the steep steps, a difficult task for him, and says in a bold, husky voice, "Bus driver! I hope you have the heat on because I'm cooolllllddd!" I love him. This stop is definitely Premium Cappuccino Chunky Chocolate.

It's true that I drive school bus in a small town. To many the people would appear to be plain vanilla. Looks can be deceiving. As a bus driver I get treated to many different flavors every day.

15 - SOMETIMES YOU HAVE TO BE A REBEL

The end of the school year makes for a busy bus driving schedule. There are activity runs all year long, but during the last two months of school, activities multiply like rabbits. Just last week, in addition to my regular morning and afternoon runs, I had four all-day activity runs. These keep a bus driver busy, but they are good for extra money and are also a lot of fun.

On Tuesday I dropped my elementary school kids at school and stayed where I was to pick up a load of first graders fifteen minutes later. Out they came in a line following a teacher. There were lots of parents with them acting as chaperones. First graders are sweet. Their innocence is refreshing. The destination was downtown Salt Lake City. I never look forward to Salt Lake City trips. There is the congested freeway, narrow city streets, unexpected one-way roads, railway tracks, and no parking—in a school bus it's a challenging obstacle course.

I dropped the kids and their adults off at Discovery Gateway and then began the next mission: find a place to park the bus for a couple of hours. This is downtown Salt Lake City. There is no open space and parking is a lucrative business. I finally found a parking lot kitty-corner to Temple Square. This lot was not meant for buses but it was largely empty that morning. I had to squeeze between two cement posts at the entrance and then park using slightly more than two parking stalls. I paid for two stalls for two hours and made my way to beautiful Temple Square. There I enjoyed two hours of reading among the blossoming trees and flowers next to the historic buildings. Moments like those are a perk of bus driving.

At noon I picked up the kids and we made our way out of the congestion of the Salt Lake Valley to the slightly less congested Utah Valley. We found a park in Lehi where we could eat our sack lunches. The kids and adults scattered about the lawn in groups in the dappled sunshine under the trees. One of my regular kids called to me from her group, "Hi, Tory." Some of my regular kids in other groups heard her and called to me, too. "Hi, Tory!" chirps out from various groups of kids like crickets on a summer evening. That is another perk of being a bus driver—the fame.

After eating, the kids ran off to the playground and mixed with kids from other schools who were already there. I wondered how the teachers would ever get them unmixed. When it was time to go I heard a whistle and then saw a stampede of kids heading my way. Those teachers have trained the kids well. We got back to the school just in time to drop the kids and then reload for the afternoon run.

On Wednesday it was much the same. I took the third grade to a Utah history museum in Lehi. Parking was slightly easier and much less expensive. I spent the two hours enjoying the museum with the kids and their adults. Quite often, between docent sessions, I would have a fresh-faced third grader sidle up to me, tell me a few things about his day, and then move on. Afterwards we went to the very same park to eat our sack lunches. The third-graders weren't quite as sweet as the first-graders. They are far more complex. I ate lunch with a group of them that included a couple of my regular riders and observed the beginnings of social pressure at work among them. I see cliques of kids and those who aren't a part. I hear kids using turns of phrases that are cool for a few weeks. But mostly, I see kids having fun. Once again we got back to the school just in time to unload and reload for the afternoon run.

On Friday I took the fifth grade to the Monte L. Bean Life Science Museum on BYU campus. In my head we would drop the kids in the parking lot behind the museum and then park there. Reality was much different. There was a women's conference on campus with thousands of attendees and their cars. Multiple busloads of kids from other schools were visiting the museum. There was a state track meeting with thousands of attendees using the BYU facilities. In other words, the campus was bursting at the seams with energy and activity. My first, second, and third parking lot choices were full. As I drove down toward the BYU stadium I saw the biggest convention of school buses I had ever seen in my life. Luckily there was room for one more. I negotiated the tight corners and made my way in. I swung that bus around and backed it in between two other buses. Success. It's always a relief to find a place to put a bus for a couple of hours.

Picking up the kids was tricky. The lot behind the museum was clogged with parked cars and other buses. With some backing I maneuvered through a turnaround that was too small for buses. Then I pretty much blocked the lane in front of the museum while waiting for my kids to load. I'm not one for breaking rules or being an inconvenience to others, but sometimes you have to be a rebel to be a school bus driver. I took the kids to Pioneer Park to eat their lunch. I detected the beginnings of middle school attitudes in the kids' conversations as they ate, but then watched them hang happily from monkey bars and swing with glee.

On Saturday I picked up the high school track team at 5:45 am. Ugh, that's an early Saturday morning. I have to give credit to the kids' commitment. I drove them up to BYU and parked in the same lot I'd found the day before. Knowing the parking layout in advance removes a lot of the bus driving anxiety. I was the second bus there, beating the other fifty two. The track meet would last all day. This was a real boon for me. I rarely get an "all-day" to myself. After parking my bus I stopped for a breakfast bagel and then climbed the hill to the main campus. The BYU Harold B. Lee Library was waiting just for me. I spent a sweet eight hours on the fifth floor writing chapter 28 of my novel. I relished every minute of so much writing time.

At 5:00 pm I walked the mile-and-a-half back to my bus to drop my computer off and then made my way to the track. An hour-and-a-half later, after some exciting races, we were loaded up and heading home. All in all the trip took fourteen hours. I enjoy the track kids. There is a quality about them that makes them attractive. Most of them aren't champions (as in first, second, or third place) and yet they work their butts off in practice and are willing to get up at 5:00 am on a Saturday morning for a meet anyway. Often I hear some talking about making their PR (personal record) that day. Yes, they are inspiring.

So that was the week of a school bus driver. It was filled with challenges, interesting places, and beautiful faces. When people find out that I, a healthy middle-aged man, drive a school bus, I see a little confusion on their faces. Should they feel sorry for me and come up with positive words to help me feel good about myself? I personally think they should envy me. I fully respect the doctors, lawyers, and insurance salespeople out there. I have a master's degree; I understand. But driving a school bus and writing books makes me happy. I guess I'm just a rebel.

16 - FIGHTING THE MUNDANE

Every weekday morning at 6:50 I arrive at my first stop. The doors hiss open and the same kids get on. I repeat this for eighteen stops. Every afternoon at 2:30 p.m. we do it again, but going the other direction. With a few exceptions it's difficult to tell one day from the next. The routine risks becoming mundane. When a job becomes mundane the employee as well as the customers suffer. I refuse to let boredom ruin this job for me and my kids.

In the afternoons I arrive at the elementary school ten or fifteen minutes before the bell rings. The bus is quiet then, but I know that in a few minutes the bell will ring and seventy hyper kids will come running toward my bus. I grab my juggling cubes and stand beside the bus and juggle. This successfully helps keep my mind off the coming chaos. The kids love it, too. I only juggle until the first kids, usually kindergarteners, arrive. They giggle and want to try it, too.

Loading in the afternoon after school is a difficult time. It takes about ten minutes for all the kids to arrive and find their seats. It's a very long ten minutes because when the engine's not running the kids want to use the bus as a playground. It takes a lot of energy on my part to keep the kids from reaching critical mass.

The bus right next to mine is supposed to wait for me to leave the loading zone first. For some reason it takes me longer to get my kids settled than it does her. If she has to wait for me very long after the usual leave time she will let her bus roll forward a foot, then stop. She will repeat this as if to say, "What the heck are you doing over there. Let's go!" I've been trying much harder to get my kids settled faster. One thing that has helped is the countdown. "Thirty seconds!" I call out over the intercom. I repeat this at twenty seconds. At ten seconds I start counting each number. Often the kids on the bus join in: 10, 9, 8, 7 . . . as they hurry to their seats. I have the bus in gear and the parking brake off so that when we get to "0" we begin to roll and all the kids cheer.

The afternoon run seems much longer than the morning run. The routine is monotonous: hit my flashers, set the brake, put the transmission in neutral, open the door, and then wait for some kids to file off. To combat this routine I started naming the stops and calling them out over the intercom as we approach. It makes it feel like a subway.

For some reason the hill on 4th East is known as Turkey Hill. I've started calling it Turkey Trot Stop. Anymore, kids expect my announcements. I asked a boy I didn't recognize which is his stop. He responded "Turkey Trot." The other day I heard some kids calling out "Grand Central" right before I was going to say it. They even mimicked my voice. Up to twenty high school and middle school kids get off at Grand Central. The next stop is Sadie's Stop. It's named after the one cute little first grader who gets off there. If I ever forget to announce it she calls it out for me. Another stop is Towhead Plaza because three platinum blonde siblings get off there. There's Dairy Cream Station at the dairy stop, and Churchyard Gang at the church parking lot.

One of my favorites is the very last house on the route when there is only one little gal on the bus. When I look in my mirror I usually can't see her. I know she's back there somewhere behind one of those tall seatbacks. "Jaida Junction," I announce. She pops up from halfway back. "Thank you," she sings out without looking at me as she plunks down each step and glides up her driveway.

Quite late into the year I handed out the "Bus Rules" papers that require parents' signatures. How likely is it that a bus driver can hand a paper to students and expect to get them back? Every week I sweep up a considerable amount of "thrown away" homework papers from the bus floor. One bus driver told me she offered candy to those who bring them back. I handed out the sheets as students got off at each stop. They rolled their eyes unenthusiastically as I made them wait to get their copy. I told them there would be a reward if they brought them back. I heard a third grader say the reward would probably be just a fun size candy bar. It was just after Halloween when he had gotten a hundred fun-size candy bars. He didn't sound motivated. I decided to take out a loan and buy full-size Hershey bars to raise the motivation factor. The next morning about a third of the kids brought their papers back. My gamble worked. Their eyes lit up when they were able to pull a full-size Hershey Bar out of the container. The other kids were hitting themselves on the forehead for not bringing theirs. I heard a lot of bargaining in the dark behind me, "I'll give you a quarter for a bite." Those papers kept coming in all week and I made sure I had candy bars ready.

The problem is now the kids are expecting me to have full-size candy bars all the time. I've learned that it isn't such a problem—it's actually useful and fun. Isaiah, an eighth grader who looks like life has been weighing a little heavy on him lately, got off at second-to-last stop. As he passed me he said, "Do you think I could have a candy bar just for being me, today?" I gave him one. As we pulled onto the gravel road that leads to the dairy an eight-year-old girl saw her family van coming down the road to the dairy from the other direction.

"That's my mom," she said with a proud smile. "I called her and she is going to give me a ride home today. Usually she won't do that."

This girl, her siblings and cousins, usually have to walk a half mile from the dairy up a hill to where their homes are. After she got off the bus I called her back to the driver's window and handed her a candy bar. "This is for your mom," I said. "She deserves one." Instead of being disappointed that the candy bar wasn't for her, she smiled brightly at the prospect of handing it over to her mom.

Tomorrow morning at 6:50 I'll be opening the door at that first stop for the eightieth time this year. I am determined that somewhere in the a.m. or p.m.run I will find some fun. Maybe someone will need a candy bar. Maybe I'll finally juggle three items with one hand. One of the kids might come to the front and ask me to tell them a story on that long stretch out in the country. I might get one of the high school kids to smile in the two seconds it takes for him to pass my seat.

17 - WHEN VALENTINE'S DAY EXPLODES

I'm trying to remember Valentine's Days of my youth. Nothing substantial comes to mind except for a Valentine's Day when I was in the second grade. We were each to bring a homemade valentine box to class and enough valentines for everyone. My mom made my box for me. It was covered in shiny tin foil and had some colorful trimmings. I thought it was beautiful. In class there was a vote for the best valentine's box. The teacher stood by the boxes and counted the hands raised of those who voted for it. Mine was one of the first. Very few voted for it. This hurt my feelings so much I decided not to vote for anyone else's box. I don't remember second grade fondly. Thanks a lot Valentine's Day.

Valentine's Day was on a Saturday this year. On the Friday morning run I noticed many of my elementary kids getting on the bus with colorful valentine boxes. There were pink boxes with hearts; red boxes with *LOVE* printed on the outside; and this being a rural town, there was even a hunter's camouflage box. The boy who sits in the front had a Minecraft-themed box. Many of the students had bags of valentines they would be handing out. I could feel a warm excitement among the kids that took me back. I must have had better Valentine's Days after second grade because the feeling of excitement I felt brought on Déjà vu. I can't remember details, but I've felt that tingly feeling on Valentine's Days of yore. It came from the hope of getting a special valentine from some cute girl I liked, or perhaps it was from the anxiety of giving a special valentine to someone who I wasn't sure felt the same way about me. Today on the bus I reveled in the feeling. The morning seemed light and happy.

I radioed one of the other bus drivers who I knew had a load of elementary kids. "Are your kids getting on the bus with pretty valentine boxes, too?"

"Yes, yes, they are," she responded. She didn't sound as delighted. I put this down to her familiarity with the day. She had been driving for over twenty years and had seen as many Valentine's Days come and go.

That afternoon the kids came running from the school and filed onto the bus. I still felt an excitement among them, but it wasn't as charming as it was that morning. Most didn't have their boxes with them now. I suspected they had thrown them away. What they did have with them was a backpack full of candy. The candy I remember from my elementary days was a few heart-shaped suckers, maybe a piece of chocolate, and lots of little hearts with *Be Mine* and *True Love* written on them. Times have changed. The kids were eating cupcakes, candy bars, sugar cookies and every other incarnation of sugar you can think of. I commented to another bus driver over the radio, "It's like Halloween, but pink."

The kids bounced around the bus like Mexican jumping beans. After unloading the last kid I drove the blessedly silent bus back to the compound. I unlatched my seatbelt and turned around to walk my bus. I stopped in astonishment—it was like Valentine's Day had exploded. Candy wrappers were still fluttering to the floor like colorful snowflakes. Now I knew why the bus driver I had spoken with that morning was a little reserved about this special day of love.

I grabbed my broom and began the chore of sweeping between and under each seat. I swept all the trash into the middle aisle before sweeping toward the front.. On this day, as I looked at the bank of trash down the aisle, I thought I might need to get a snow shovel to finish the job. I eventually got the residue of Valentine's Day out of my bus. It was a lot of work, and I'm annoyed that the kids can throw their wrappers on the floor without a second thought. Even after all this, I'm surprised to find that I'm still looking forward to seeing the colorful boxes next year. I suppose I'm just sentimental.

18 - BAD TRIPS

School bus drivers have their regular morning and afternoon routes. They pick up and drop off the same kids morning and afternoon every school day of the year. It's very routine. I find myself looking forward to special activity trips that give me a break from the usual. These trips might be anything from driving the volleyball team to a match to taking the sixth graders to a natural history museum. However, not all activity trips are equal.

An easy activity trip is one that takes you to a place with little traffic and lots of parking space. I find the majority of activity trips for our school district fit the easy category to one degree or another. I drove to Mt. Pleasant the other day. I was able to drop the team at the front doors of the high school and then drive to the public library. I parked the bus along the curb where there was plenty of room. After a couple of hours of writing I had a bite to eat at the diner across the street. I drove back to the school in time to catch the varsity match before bringing the kids home. It was a pleasant trip.

Then there are the bad trips. On one of these I drove the cross country team to Park City up in the mountains for a large meet. The difficulty of this trip didn't lie with the kids. I like driving the cross country team. They are focused, well-mannered kids and are fun to watch run. It was the venue that made this trip so disagreeable.

Another bus driver had told me about her experience a couple of years before. The venue has absolutely no parking for buses. She dropped the team at the venue, just outside of town, and then drove to the high school where she had been told there was parking available. The difficulty is that the high school is difficult to recognize. It is built in conjunction with a performing arts center and happens to look like the arts center—not a high school. She had gotten lost looking for the high school and found herself on the extremely narrow roads on the hillside of this charming old mining town all the while needing to find a bathroom. Once, after dropping a load off at a museum, I found myself on narrow one-lane roads above a university set on a mountainside, so I took her story to heart.

I dropped the team off at the venue via a narrow two-lane road with two little parking lots just barely big enough to turn a bus around. These lots wouldn't accommodate two buses let alone the thirty that would be arriving. I went searching for the high school which was supposed to be about a mile up the road. I saw a bus in front of me and decided to follow it hoping that the driver had been here before. I was right that the driver had been here before. I was wrong in assuming he was going to the high school. I followed him into a school complex where I saw eight buses already parked. They were parked nose to tail very closely, which was unusual, but I thought, "This must be how they do it here." Then I noticed that all the buses were from the local school district. To my horror I realized that I was in the bus pickup line for an elementary school. Kids were streaming out of the school and getting on the buses. Local bus drivers are ornery about other-district drivers getting in their way, so I quickly looked for a way out. All I could manage was to pull to the side in some empty car parking spots where there was barely enough room. Local bus drivers glanced my way as they eased past me into the loading lanes, but otherwise they tried to pretend I wasn't there. I had to wait for the afternoon loading to complete before I could leave.

After I finally made my escape, I drove toward town worried that I was going to miss the high school and end up on one of those narrow mountainside roads my friend had told me about. I saw a few buses parked in front of a building that did not look like a high school. The parking lot was full of cars, but there was a curb with enough room for my bus. I pulled in not caring if it was the high school or not, and parked. I got out to reconnoiter and did a little jig when I found out this was the elusive high school. Now there would be a four-hour wait.

I was just getting my laptop set up to do a little writing on my bus when a man came to tell me and the other bus drivers who had made their way there to park somewhere else because they needed this curb for the bus that would shuttle people to the meet. He had no suggestions for where we should park. I found room around on the other side of the performing arts center with fourteen other buses parked higgledy-piggledy amid the cars. The transportation planning was very poor for such a large meet. Normally I like to find a good place to watch the kids run and cheer them on, but because we had to park so far away from the venue I had to sit this one out on the bus. I read a book, took a nap, and walked around the parking lot for exercise.

After four hours I got a call from one of the coaches. He wanted me to get there fast, "And, for heaven's sake, stay out of the line of buses on that narrow road." If I got into that line it would take an hour-and-a-half to cycle through. I understood his concern, but how else was I supposed to pick up the team? It seemed the only other alternative was to park on the busy four-lane highway and have the team come to me. But that was far too dangerous. As I approached the venue I saw a possibility and formulated a strategy. The plan required a couple of difficult U-turns. After the U-turns I parked on an unused sidewalk with three other buses that had had the same idea. I called the coach and the team came to me. Due to my creativity we got home an hour-and-a-half sooner. While the time savings was convenient my conscience weighed on me; I didn't like what I had to do to accomplish the task. If I make that run again I'll have to figure something else out or just wait in line.

The coaches showed a little appreciation for my efforts, but not nearly enough. I would have accepted a ticker-tape parade down Main Street.

I told my story to some of the more veteran bus drives. In return I got "bad trip" stories that made me look like a punk complainer: breakdowns at midnight 150 miles from home, waiting two hours for a tow truck to pull a bus out of a snowbank, getting into spots where she couldn't turn around or back out. If bad trips were monsters, it turns out my monster run was more of a six-year-old under a sheet as a ghost than a true Frankenstein.

19 - MUSIC OF THE DAY

My daughter, a high school senior, likes to sleep as much as any other teenager. I have seen her get out of bed at noon. Even so, she can get up early when she needs to. Last Friday I was to pick up the high school choir and band at 7:00 am. My daughter, a member of the choir, got up extra early to be with me while I fueled the bus and performed the pre-trip inspection. I pulled into the loading zone and engaged the parking brake with its *hushhh*. As soon as I opened the doors sleepy-eyed high school students began boarding. They carried music folders, instruments, blankets, and bags filled with snacks. One student lugged in a double-bass that was bigger than him. A girl followed, hugging her green-frog pillow close. Like all good high school students they gravitated toward the back of the bus. The double-bass got the coveted last two seats. Those students who were planning on sleeping chose seats in the middle of the bus where it would be quieter.

Finally everyone was loaded—except for one. He hadn't arrived.

"I know he's in bed asleep," said the choir director in a resigned voice. "Anyone have his number?"

Someone in the back of the bus yelled, "He doesn't have a phone. Neither does his house."

"What?" Several people including the choir director asked disbelievingly.

The choir director hesitated a moment, then, in a determined voice, she said, "Let's go get him."

In my forty-foot taxi we drove across town and up his street. I braked to a stop in front of his home and popped the air brake. The hiss sounded extra loud on the sleeping street.

"I have an air horn," I said, reaching for the cord. I was mostly teasing. All the houses on the street were dark, including the neighboring house with the highway patrol car parked out front.

The choir director raised an eyebrow at my suggestion. "Let's just send someone to knock on the door," she said The boy we were missing was on the football team. We sent out a fellow team member. We could hear him pounding on the door over the idling engine. Eventually a light turned on and the door opened. I caught a glimpse of a long nightgown. We had waked his mother. Not two minutes later the sleeping beauty came bounding onto the bus with his favorite red-fuzzy pillow. His classmates cheered. With him now on board, we were off on our eighty-mile journey. These students had been selected to be a part of the honor choir and band along with top musicians of nine other schools.

In Richfield I dropped the band students at the high school. I took the choir students a few blocks south to the middle school. This brought back memories. Thirty-three years earlier I had been in the high school band and choir. A bus driver had dropped me off at All-State events for a day of music. Back then, I hadn't foreseen the day when I would be driving a bus and seeing the face of my seventeen-year-old daughter in the rear-view mirror among the other kids.

It must be strange when your dad is the bus driver for a high school trip. If he was cool-looking maybe it would be all right. I'm not so cool-looking. I've got a flattop haircut and a pot belly. My fashion sense is lacking and my clothes are non-descript. My daughter doesn't seem to mind even though she is beautiful and fashionable. Once, our eyes met when I glanced in the rear-view mirror. She smiled at me.

I loaded the students for lunch and dropped them off at a shopping center where there were lots of places to eat. I didn't have any cash to give my daughter for lunch and I wasn't going to give her my debit card. She was going to have to stay with me if she wanted to eat. I saw a Pizza Hut and told my daughter we would eat there. I love Pizza Hut's Pepperoni Lover's pizza. When the last person got off the bus, I shut the door and turned to find my daughter and six other kids.

"Looks like we have a group, Daddy," she said, happily.

I hadn't expected this. Instead of the nice, quiet lunch with my daughter I would be the adult tag-along to her and her friends. Actually, I like being with groups of teens. I feel comfortable with them. At first they don't seem as comfortable with me. I have to accept the fact that they're uncomfortable with their friends' fathers. I thought I was prepared to stay quiet during lunch and let them do their thing, but I just couldn't. When our server spilled a tray of six drinks at our table, conversation opened up. I probably talked too much, but I got to know my daughter's friends a little better. My daughter, who sat next to me, didn't appear concerned.

On the way back to the bus my daughter laughed as she told me, "Some of the kids knew you were my dad. Others had to figure it out. They were wondering why I'm hanging with the bus driver."

It was eight o'clock when they finished their evening rehearsal. It was very dark outside. I had the bus going and the lights on when the kids started boarding. Somewhere in the middle of the line my daughter climbed on. She stopped the line long enough to kiss me on the cheek. That kiss made a rather plain, middle-aged man with a flattop feel like a million dollars. It was like she was asking the other students, "Don't you wish your Dad were here?"

I had sat in on the choir's evening rehearsal. The guest conductor was very talented. He pulled the kids together and drew beautiful music from their throats and hearts. I felt lucky to witness this coming together of voices and souls. It was on the long drive home that the music of the day became even more beautiful. My daughter felt like talking to me. She moved up to the seat right behind mine. For eighty miles I heard the music of her voice in my right ear as we chatted about the things on her mind. All of the kids had had a wonderful experience throughout the day. For me, it was the best school trip ever.

20 - ZEN AND THE ART OF BUS DRIVING

What do I know about Zen? I know how to spell it. I know about Zen gardens: some sand, a rock, and a little rake to make lines. I've read *Zen and the Art of Motorcycle Maintenance*. So, actually, I know very little about Zen, but I do know a little about school bus driving.

I've learned that school bus driving isn't for the faint of heart. In saying this I don't want to mislead you. School bus driving isn't particularly dangerous. The children in our district don't seem prone to violence or delinquency; but five days every week a school bus driver has to face the fact that for two to four hours a day his will alone stands as the barrier between order and universal chaos.

From my college freshman physics class I learned that the law of entropy has to do with ordered states naturally moving into disordered states. The law of entropy is especially apparent on school buses. On a normal day I can feel the energy on the bus contained in the kids behind me bending the space-time continuum. It is my presence, and my presence alone, that keeps a singularity from occurring. This is hardly fair. When Yoda or Professor Charles Xavier confronts the forces of chaos and destruction they get to do so with their full attention. School bus drivers have to confront these forces while keeping both eyes on the road. Could Yoda wield his light-sabre so magnificently while safely driving a school bus? I don't think so.

In my imagination I've looked up into the mirror to see sixty-five students sitting correctly in their seats, talking quietly and happily to each other as they await their stop. In reality I will look into my mirror to see kindergarteners standing on their seats facing the back, middle-schoolers with knees and heads out in the aisles so they can conference with kids on the other side of the bus, and high schoolers sitting high in their seats with their backs against the windows. Third graders will be singing about chickens farting, a fifth grader will be walking up the aisle to get a tissue, and hidden behind one of those tall seatbacks a fourth grade boy will be having a screaming contest with a fourth grade girl. This is what happens on a good day.

First and foremost a school bus driver has to worry about what is happening on the road. Other cars and trucks pose the greatest danger to the kids. In an accident the kids have the potential of becoming flying objects injuring themselves and others. Sitting in their seats lessens this possibility somewhat. Ironically, trying to minimize the "flying object" risk inside the bus increases the collision risk outside the bus by taking the bus drivers attention off the road.

My greatest challenge is trying to find an inner peace in equilibrium with the energy on the bus so that I can remain aware of what is going on outside the bus. Some days I achieve what I call the Zen Zone. With quick glances in the mirror and efficient use of the intercom I am able to keep the human combustion on the bus reasonably contained while being aware of the car unexpectedly braking in front of me. Other days the Zen Zone is harder to achieve. I become a surly curmudgeon snapping at the rule-breakers over the intercom while giving the road short shrift. Twice on these kinds of days I have grabbed the radio microphone instead of the intercom microphone and told all the other bus drivers to "turn around and sit down and don't make me ask you again."

The bad days happen when I start taking what is happening on the bus personally. Billy will suddenly leap into the aisle and meet my eyes in the mirror. He knows the rule about staying out of the aisle. He's been told of the danger. Yet, for no apparent reason, he steps into the aisle and stares at me. Is this not a personal challenge? Ironically, a simple, "Back in your seat, Billy" gets him to sit back down. Maybe his legs were cramped. Maybe he just wanted a little adult attention. I don't know. I do know that if I start taking the students' rule infractions too much to heart my driving becomes more dangerous. I tend to drive faster. I hurry to the next stop just so I can let more students off and be done with them. At a couple of stops, where I let up to seventeen off at once, I feel the same relief that comes from sitting down after a long walk. This isn't a healthy state-of-mind for a school bus driver. I've been learning that what happens on the bus really isn't about me. The kids are just living their lives. I do have to enforce rules now and then to keep chaos at bay, but mostly all that energy is being dissipated in friendly talk and laughter.

I carry quite a load of middle schoolers. There is a lot of angst amongst this group. Most of them seem afraid to be seen talking to me. They won't even return a 'hello.' They walk by and look the other way just as they reach me.

There are two girls who get off together at one stop. Every day I say, "Bye" or "See you tomorrow" only to be ignored. I've seen them put their heads close together as they cross the street in front of the bus. I imagine they are saying "Can you believe he spoke to me? The nerve!" It's right out of a scene with the mean girls from a Disney movie.

One day I noticed that one of the girls was wearing a necklace with an old-fashioned bicycle hanging at the bottom. It caught my attention that such a young person would wear such a unique decoration. She was wearing it the next day as well. She got off alone on this day. As she passed I said, "That's a great necklace. I love the bicycle." I expected her to be offended that the bus driver liked something she wore. She mumbled something as she went down the steps. I didn't catch what it was. As she crossed in front of the bus she ignored me as usual, but I saw her smile slightly and touch her necklace. Maybe she was pleased to have her necklace noticed? We're not going to be friends anytime soon, but it made me feel good to know she heard me and didn't resent it.

Today a third grade boy walked up the aisle at one of our stops and handed me a ticket. It was from the Police Department. Apparently I was in an oversize vehicle and the fine was $10,000. This would have disturbed me if the ticket wasn't written on a lined sheet of paper torn out of a pocket notebook. It also helped that it was written in pencil in third grade handwriting. Do the creators of this ticket have it in for me? Are they wishing me ill? I can't tell for sure, but the truth is I enjoyed their creativity. I saw them in the mirror watching me as I read the ticket. They were delighted by my mock consternation.

I drive more slowly now whether the bus is quiet or loud. Every once in a while I have to call a kid on a stunt he or she pulls, but mainly the noise I am hearing behind me is just the noise of kids growing up. I am capable of giving someone the "eye" to influence them to "stop it," but I am just as capable of being a cheerful "hello" and a "smile" in their day whether they like it or not.

21 - GAMES WE PLAY

Yes, we will walk with a walk that is measured and slow
And we will go where the chalk white arrows go
For the children they mark and the children they know
The place where the sidewalk ends.

That is the last stanza to Shel Silverstein's poem, "Where the Sidewalk Ends." Aria just repeated it to me along with the preceding stanzas.

"Did I get it?" she asked.

I dug out a king-size Butterfinger candy bar and gave it to her.

"Really?" she said. She took the candy bar and skipped her way back to her seat.

Aria learned to take advantage of my little games a long time ago. When I look in my rear-view mirror during the afternoon run and see all those unfocused kids making so much noise it makes me want to do something with them. But what can a bus driver do? The job is simply to get them safely where they are supposed to go. That involves keeping both eyes on the road and a third eye watching their behavior in the mirror.

One day an idea slipped into my head. I challenged one of the children as she got off the bus to do something nice for someone she didn't know very well and to do it anonymously. She came back a day later and reported what she had done. I gave her a Hershey's chocolate bar. Other kids found out about this and wanted in. I typed up the challenge and made them write down what they did before I would give them the candy bar. They brought back bits of paper with wobbly print describing how they had written a note to someone and hidden it in her desk or said something nice to a boy at lunch.

"Give me another challenge," Aria said.

I thought for a couple of days and came up with the "Letter Writing Challenge." They were to write a letter with actual pen and paper and snail-mail it to the recipient. They had to describe the stamp they put on the envelope to me. I thought this would be something they hadn't done before. Several took the challenge and earned a Payday or a 100,000 Grand bar. Then there was the "Do the Dishes When It Isn't Your Turn" challenge. That wasn't as hard as I thought it might be for some of them. They have good parents.

Only a few kids were participating in the challenges and I wanted to get other kids involved. I came up with the Question of the Day. I got on the intercom one morning just before we got to the elementary school and asked, "What's the square root of 64?" I thought they would have to go look that up. Several didn't. They knew it and it cost me several candy bars. I had to make things a little harder or I was going to go broke. I came up with questions that would require a little research.

As we pulled into the bus zone at their school I got on the intercom and asked, "What is the capital of Azerbaijan?"

They couldn't pronounce Azerbaijan so I had to repeat it several times. I thought they would ask a teacher to help them look it up. They didn't. Actually, one kid did, but he said his teacher said there was no such place. Go figure. Finally, when I asked over the intercom if anyone was ever going to get it, someone looked it up on their smartphone.

"Baku?" a girl asked, struggling with the pronunciation. We had a winner.

There were many other questions like, "What is the chemical formula to heavy water?" or," What is the deepest fresh water lake in the world?" Some of these questions hung for days before some ambitious kid became motivated enough to find the answer. When we had a winner I always announced it over the intercom and made sure everyone knew what candy bar the winner got. All the kids wanted candy bars and would beg for them when they got off the bus. If they weren't motivated enough to look up an answer they didn't get one.

I had asked some older kids to name the planets of the solar system from closest to the sun outward. They couldn't do it and lost interest. One little second-grader wanted a chance at a candy bar, but he wanted an easier question. I didn't have another question ready so I told him it would be okay if he asked his mom and dad for the answer and told me tomorrow. He was unhappy that it was a question he couldn't answer right then. He sat in the front seat near me in deep thought as we neared his stop. Then, quietly and deliberately, he began, "Mercury, Venus, Earth . . ." and went on to Pluto. My mouth dropped open.

"Did I get it?" he asked.

"Did you! How did you know that?" I asked.

He thought a moment and answered, "I don't know."

He got his candy bar.

I changed things up to memorization for the fun of it. A few kids actually memorized the first two paragraphs to the Gettysburg Address for a king-sized candy bar. Then I pulled out "Someone Ate the Baby," by Shel Silverstein. Aria balked at the length, but in the end she memorized it. Then went back and taught two other girls the poem. One-by-one they came up and recited it to me without help. It got a little annoying as they practiced. Several times they came up before they were ready to show me what they had memorized. I heard the line "Someone ate the baby," about a million times. The poor kids who sat in the front were groaning in pain before it was over. Some of them almost had it memorized even though they weren't trying.

This last poem, "Where the Sidewalk Ends", was difficult for Aria. I don't know why. It was shorter than "Someone Ate the Baby." I memorized it while walking the mile to my bus for my afternoon run. Aria struggled. Three times, after she failed to recite it, she said, "I don't want the candy bar anyway," and stomped back to her seat. Her friend decided she wanted to do it. Mara memorizes things really fast. She is gifted. One night, after Aria had stomped back to her seat again candy-bar-less, Mara almost completed the poem. I knew she would have it the next morning. When I gave her the candy bar I knew that Aria would be back up to try again.

That's exactly what happened. In the morning Mara came up, and in spite of all the noise on the bus, she recited the poem perfectly. She had to stop while we loaded more kids, but she was able to pick up where she left off and finally finish. She went back with her king-size Butterfinger. Aria came up almost immediately. She was really nervous. This was hard for her. It took her four stops, but in the end she recited it sufficiently well. She was so happy.

Not everyone wants to play my games. I don't even try with the middle and high school kids. Although one day one of the middle school girls came up to argue that an answer I had just rejected was correct. She described how she had researched the answer. I realized that she had done the research for her little sister.

"It sounds like you deserve the candy bar," I told her. "You did all the work." She looked at me like she hadn't thought of that. She accepted the candy bar. Her little sister pouted a little but got over it. Ah, the games we play.

22 - KEEP ON ANNOYING ME

The daily morning pick-ups and afternoon drop-offs are the routine of the school bus driver. It's the activity trips that spice up our job. On Thursday morning at nine a.m. I began loading thirty-five students who were on their way to the State FFA convention. The next three days were a nice break to my routine.

I live in a very small country town. Signs for Future Farmers of America (FFA) are all around me. Often there are flyers announcing events and activities. Sometimes I see kids in the iconic blue FFA jackets. Even so I know very little about the program. I picture kids raising, grooming, and selling animals. It seemed probable to me that there would be animals at the convention. When the kids started arriving to load the bus I was surprised. These weren't kids who were dressed to be working with animals—the boys were in black dress pants, white shirts, and ties; the girls wore black skirts, black tights, white blouses, and a tie. Both genders wore their short, blue FFA jackets with Mt. Nebo printed clearly on the back. They were dressed for business.

The thirty-five kids filled the bus comfortably. Many had a seat to themselves while a few others had to share. School buses aren't the most comfortable mode of travel. The high seatbacks in the newer buses like mine make it so the kids can't see those in the seats in front or behind them. So what do the kids want to do? They stand up to talk completely negating the safety feature of the padded seatbacks. Each time I loaded this group, about six times each day, I had to get on the intercom and instruct them to sit down. Surprisingly they would stay seated until the next time they loaded.

I've been on other three-day trips. On most of them I drop the kids at their venue, and, except for lunch, leave them there all day. I get to go do what I want during that time. It's like a vacation. Not on this trip. I dropped them for lunch and then picked them up an hour later. I dropped them at the venue and picked them up two hours later. I dropped them at the motel for dinner and picked them up two hours later. I dropped them at the venue for more meetings and picked them up three hours later. I dropped them at the motel so they could change into street clothes for the night's extra activity. I dropped them at the venue where they saw a hypnotist show and then picked them up at 11:15 pm for the last time that day.

The next day was much of the same back and forth. The special activity that night was a dance. It was fun to see the kids exchange their official FFA dress for their dance clothes: mainly jeans and nice button-up shirts. It was cowboy boots all around. I was able to come a bit early and look in on the dance. I watched 500 FFA kids do the Macarena. It was great.

Because this was a well-attended state event there were a multitude of school buses. It was fun to check out the school district printed on the sides of the buses to see where they came from. The district names are usually the name of the county they serve. Some of them are Wayne, Emery, and Garfield. I have no idea where in the state of Utah those buses came from. I talked to one bus driver from a rural area who picks up kids in a town thirty-five miles away from the high school. That's a long daily route. She talked of narrow misses with elk in the canyons. I talked with another bus driver who had been driving for twenty-nine years. She was confident and still pleasant after all those years. I couldn't help but feel what a rookie I was after my one year of full-time bus driving.

Parking at large events such as these is always an adventure. Quite often a natural order will develop and buses will line up beside each other across an empty stretch of parking lot. Other times buses just park helter-skelter wherever they can find space. There was a little bit of both at this venue. At the motel four of us lined up nicely on the vacant lot next door. It had a secret little lane I discovered when I dropped the kids off at the venue. It put them close to the entrance and we didn't have to line up behind the other buses. On the second day another bus driver figured it out and beat me there. Sometimes you just can't trust another bus driver.

The best part of the trip was the kids themselves. There is something invigorating about being close to youth. There was such a range of personalities that the more self-controlled kids balanced those prone to acting out.

"No swearing on the bus!" one girl called out boldly as she got on and heard some farmyard language near the back. It was gratifying to see her in action. She wasn't preaching. She was well-liked and just wanted to make the speaker be his best self. Another time amid the cacophony I heard another girl call out, "This is a G-rated bus." Not every group of kids has someone like that.

I sit in my seat and watch them pass as they load. Their faces become familiar to me. At first most avert their eyes from mine when they see me. After a few loadings and unloadings some of them will not only meet my eyes, but give me a smile or a nod. I love it when that happens. A large part of this group thanks me for the ride each time they got off. Considering I drop them sometimes six times in a day this almost gets annoying. Still, I try to give a sincere and unique response to each of them. Don't think I'm complaining about their consideration. I'm not. In fact, I hope they keep annoying me!

I was opening the bus compound gate after I had made the final drop at our high school after we returned home. The kids' parents were picking them up after their three-day adventure. As I pulled on the gate I heard a honk. I looked up to see an arm with the blue FFA jacket sleeve stretched out the window. As the car passed a voice called, "Thank you!" It had been a good trip.

23 - I TELL THEM STORIES

I was a new bus driver still trying to find the answer of how to control the kids on my bus. Imagine my disappointment when I discovered that you can't control them.

However, I did eventually learn that my relationship with the kids on my bus isn't one of a lion tamer cracking his whip. It's more like a father. A good father definitely lays down rules, but rather than force and intimidation, he uses persuasion and influence based on love to get his children to do the right thing. This may be a little saccharine for some, but the fact is that for up to two hours a day my students and I are living pretty close together and need to get along. Approaching the situation with a family perspective has been helpful to me.

Before I developed my family approach to order on the bus, I was having trouble with an eight-year-old boy. You can picture a cute, innocent little boy if you want to, but this boy could be mistaken for a twelve-year-old due to his size and manner. In the midst of all the noise on the bus there was a particular agitation about four seats back that always caught my attention. It was Steven. I'm not sure what he was doing to cause such a commotion—the high seat backs kept me from seeing—but whatever it was created a ruckus. I finally moved him to the front passenger seat to separate him from the others. He wasn't happy about this—at first.

Moving a child to the front seat is supposed to be a punishment to persuade a change in behavior. My problem is that I tend to talk to those who sit up front and this leads to becoming acquainted. I found Steven to be a lively kid with an active imagination. In the course of our conversation I told him a story. I can't remember exactly what it was about, but I'm pretty sure it was just some odd news item. He liked the story, or the way I told it, so much that he asked for another, and then another. The next day he sat in the front seat without being told to. He asked for more stories. Within a couple of days I realized he had decided to move to the front seat permanently.

I also realized I had created trouble for myself. He expected stories every day. And not only him, but some of the other kids learned something was going on in the front of the bus. Soon I could sense three faces poking up over the divider behind my seat to listen to my stories. Others leaned toward me from the front passenger seat. Twice I missed stops due to my storytelling. It became so distracting that I had to quit telling stories for a while. After a couple of days most of the kids gave up on me and went back to their regular seats. Not Steven. He stayed in the front seat. He liked talking to me, stories or not. When he got off the bus at school or his home stop he would turn around right by the door and wave. He would stand there and keep waving until I shut the door on him. No matter how many times I said no, Steven still pestered me for stories. I found a compromise by waiting until after the most chaotic part of the route was over before I started a story.

Although Steven was my main audience, and only rode in the afternoon, kids on the morning route started coming to the front and asking for a story. The morning run is so much quieter than the afternoon that it's easier to tell a story then. I spent a month telling them the story of *Joey and the Magic Map*, a novel I wrote, chapter by chapter. Every morning it was, "Okay, Tory, tell us more." I would have to remember where we left off, reformulate the chapter for a vocal telling, and for the time remaining until I dropped them off. It wasn't easy, but on the country roads with miles in between stops I could do it. After *Joey* I told them *The Graveyard Book*. Then it was the *Secret Benedict Society*. Other times I just resorted to odd news items again, or funny stories from my life.

Every once in a while I am surprised by who is asking for a story. Aiden, a fifth grader, sits near the middle of the bus. He never has much to say to me. If I say anything to him it is usually "Turn around and sit down." He tends to have an "I could care less" demeanor about him. The other day he wandered up to the front seat a few miles before we got to his stop and sat down in that casual manner of his. "Tory, tell me a story," he said. I got over my surprise and came up with something.

Another day it was little Kaye who suddenly appeared in the passenger seat. She usually resides in the middle of the bus, too. I call her little, and she is only nine, but I have learned there is a certain sophistication to nine-year-olds.

"Can you tell me a story?" she asked.

There was a wistfulness—a hopefulness—in her voice. She hadn't made the trek up front for a couple of months so her appearance surprised and pleased me a little. We were on the eight-mile stretch through junipers and sagebrush to the dairy and since there were no more than ten kids on the bus it seemed a good time for a story. I told the first chapter of the *Graveyard Book* again. She hadn't heard it yet. Three other kids moved to the front when they realized a story was happening. They listened intently as I told them about the three-year-old boy who wandered up to the graveyard one night and ended up being raised by the ghosts who lived there.

Some days the stories flow easily. Other days the energy level on the bus is too high to tell a story and I have to tell the asker no. On those days I am irritated and grumpy. Once, after a series of grumpy days a fourth grade boy in jeans and cowboy boots scooted to the front seat. He's a pickup, deer hunting kind of boy who has never paid me or my stories much interest. But he's a good kid I'm glad to have him in my bus family. He surprised me when he kicked back in the seat and asked nonchalantly, "You got a story?"

Like any dad who gets positive attention from one of his kids I perked up inside. I thought for a moment and said, "Why, yes. Yes, I do."

24 - THINGS HEARD AND SEEN

A bus driver's job is full of sound bites and video clips. I hear pieces of conversations as kids pass getting on or off. As we are driving I hear things shouted above the normal din that makes me wonder. I glance up in the mirror and see things I don't always understand. Some days I wonder if wearing ear plugs and blinders would make my job easier.

Buses will always be noisy if you have very many kids. School kids are social, and for most the bus ride is a social time. But there is noise and then there is *NOISE*. Noise is the sound of fifty to sixty kids talking and laughing. *NOISE* is the sound of two boys four seats back screaming like the banshee that terrified me as a child in *Darby O'Gill and the Little People*. I want to tell them that we don't need a portent of Death on board, but they wouldn't understand. I settle for telling them to shut it.

NOISE is the little Hispanic boy calling "TORYEES! TORYEES" repeatedly until I am forced to answer. My name is Tory, but for some reason that is the way he hears it. I already know what he is going to say. In the all-seeing rear-view mirror I have been watching him poke his face around the edge of his seat again and again while the girl sitting there tries to backhand it like in Whack-A-Mole. She finally got him.

NOISE is the continual farting sounds made with mouths against arms that comes from three seats back. I have been known to be entertained by bathroom humor, but these noises go on and on and on until even an aficionado like me can't stand it anymore. When I finally make them stop with the fart noises, the "pee" and "wiener" talk starts up.

These boys are brother and cousins. The oldest of them, who is nine, loves to bully the younger two who are seven. Bully may be too strong a word for it since the younger two enjoy it as much as the bigger boy. When I pull into the stop in the morning the little boys are attacking the big boy and he is collaring them and pulling them into bear hugs. They have the biggest smiles on their faces. They continue this wrestling on the bus. Finally I have to separate them. This is a difficult decision. You see, these boys *love* to sit by each other and wrestle. They are the happiest kids on the bus when they sit together. By separating them I took 80% of the fun factor out of their bus ride. I do separate them, though. I get over the guilt.

The things I see aren't nearly as bad as what I hear. The worst thing I see is the face of kids getting on or off the bus with *attitude*. The attitude lasts only as long as they are passing me. We don't even know each other, but as the bus driver and an adult I am their natural enemy. At least that's how they see it. Why else would they turn their heads away when I say 'hello' or 'have a good day?' These are usually middle school or high school kids. Most aren't this way, but there are a few who always have that annoyed look on their face when they pass me.

One afternoon there were only five kids left on the bus. We were heading to the dairy where almost everyone who rides the bus is a sibling or a cousin. I looked in the mirror to see a boy standing in the back with a tennis shoe in his hand holding it up to his cousin's nose. She sniffed it cautiously before making a face. They both broke up in laughter. I don't understand.

Sometimes after the dairy there is one little girl left on the bus. She would take exception at being called little. She is a sixth grader going on senior in high school, but she still looks like a little girl. Usually it is just she and me on the bus for the last eight miles. She only rides the bus home half the time. Because of the high seats I can't see if she is on the bus or not, so after the Dairy Cream Gang gets off she will usually raise her hand and call out casually "I'm here."

On this particular day she called out "We're here." She had a friend coming home to play with her. I'm sure she would prefer the word *hang*. About four miles into the back roads to her home I look in the mirror to see four bare feet resting on top of a seat. That was the only sign of them.

One day a third grader stuck his head into the aisle and the following conversation occurred:

Boy: "Tory."

Me: "Yeah?"

Boy: "It's my birthday."

Me: "Happy Birthday!"

Boy: "But nobody got me anything."

Me: "That's sad."

Boy: "Well, they got me a shirt."

Me: "That's a good gift."

Boy: "But it was a dirty shirt."

At this point I realized the third grader was performing a comedy routine.

One morning the kids were particularly sleepy. The bus was quiet save for the engine and tire noise. It was winter and the sun was not yet up. Somewhere from the middle of the bus I hear a child's voice call out, "Step on it, Tory."

On a long stretch of highway to one of my stops I spotted a sixty-four ounce fountain drink cup lying in my lane. I positioned the bus hoping to squash it with my tires. I smiled with satisfaction when I heard the crunch. Then I heard a low, slow chuckle down by my elbow. I looked to see one of my second grade girls peeking around the partition with a grin on her face and a sparkle in her dark eyes. She had seen the whole thing and approved.

One warm spring afternoon I heard screaming in the back. I looked up to see six kids leaping for the other side of the bus. Their windows were down and apparently a strong stream of water from a farmer's circular irrigation system had been perfectly timed with our passing. The kids looked at me with laughing, accusing eyes like I had done that on purpose. I hadn't, but I didn't deny it—that would have taken the fun out of it.

Recently a little gal gave me a post-it note telling me I was the best bus driver ever. She had drawn a picture of a bus with me and her in front of it. I stuck this note on my side panel. It's still there reminding me that I see and hear far more good on the bus than bad.

25 - LUCKY

Special activity runs range from overnight trips in distant towns for sporting tournaments to a two-block drive to the school district office so the choir can perform at a luncheon. These special activity runs have taken me to towns I never would have seen and to events I never would have experienced. I enjoy these events as much as the students do.

Girls' soccer is a new sporting event at our high school. When I drove the soccer girls they were still classified as a club instead of a team. The first time I drove the girls to a match the acting coach told me that this was the second time most of them had ever played a match. I don't have much interest in soccer and, in spite of the sunshine, the wind was nippy that afternoon. I stayed on the bus and read a book for a while. Then curiosity got the better of me. I raised the hood on my hoodie, zipped it up to my chin, and ventured out of the bus to see how the girls were doing. The score was 3-0 when I arrived at the field. Our girls were losing. I didn't have to watch long before I was impressed, in spite of the score, at the teamwork of our girls. They were passing well and showed a lot of hustle and determination. If they were cold, and I'm sure they were, they didn't show it.

On the bus after the game one of the girls asked the coach what the final score was.

"5-0," she answered.

"Again?" another girl said.

"My dad came to the game," the coach said. "He asked, 'This is their second game?'"

"Was that a good thing?" a girl asked.

"Yes! He thought you were playing far better than such an inexperienced team."

The girls, five-to-zero losers, cheered.

It was dark by the time we headed home. It was even darker being on a remote highway on a moonless night. The darkness was lightened by the strains of music coming from the back of the bus. The music wasn't from an MP3 player or an iPad—it was from the girls themselves. Several of the soccer club girls were in the concert choir. They were singing choir songs in harmony. You don't get that when you drive boy teams. The only selection I ever heard from the boys was when the track team sang "One Hundred Bottles of Beer on the Wall." They didn't miss a bottle.

I took a group of boys to a summer basketball tournament in a town located four hours away. I picked them up two days later. It was hot. Really hot. The temperature was 114 degrees. School buses don't have air conditioning. As we started the journey home most of the windows were down. We hadn't gone five miles before the boys shut the windows. The wind coming in the window was so hot it was slightly less miserable to bake with them shut. There were plenty of seats up front, but high school students are drawn to the back of the bus like moths to a porch light. The bus engine is in the back. This raised the temperature in the back ten degrees compared to the front of the bus. I told the boys this, but they wouldn't move up. Instead, a few of them just took their clothes off. They sat there in their underwear sweating profusely. The bus overheated three times and we had to stop to cool the engine. By the time we got home the boys were melted over the seats like the clocks in Salvador Dali's "Persistence of Memory." Well, almost like that.

One day I drove choir members to a regional competition. At this competition the kids sang in duets, quartets, and octets. Eventually the choirs would compete. While the kids waited for the choir competition to begin they hung out in the gym. There happened to be a keyboard and a basketball present. A few kids, in their tuxedos and concert dresses, took up the basketball and started shooting hoops. Another boy sat down at the keyboard and started to bang out music the choir had practiced. He started with "A Bridge Over Troubled Water." A few kids circled the piano and started to sing. Soon more ran over to join in. They moved on to more difficult and more sacred pieces. They ended with "Jabberwocky," a silly, but very difficult piece. By then most of the choir was present. There was no audience and no choir director. The kids were singing for the sheer joy of singing. They sang in each other's faces and acted out the parts—all things they couldn't do on stage. The joy and fun of it was palpable. Even the choir members who were playing basketball were singing along as they shot the ball.

I've driven the wrestlers, the girls' basketball team, the boys and girls' track teams, the drama club, and elementary school field trips to dairies and zoos, just to name a few. I've had many memorable trips along with a couple of nightmares. The trip I had the most fun on was the concert choir to state competition. The location was good for the choir (a concert hall on the University of Utah campus), but bad for bus drivers. After dropping the choir at the venue it was every bus driver for himself to find a place to park. It was congested and the streets were narrow in that part of the city. I ended up cramming my bus between two driveways in a residential neighborhood, then waited for two hours. The fun didn't occur until we got back to our fair, little town. Our high is a small-town high school classified 2-A. In the arts it has to compete against the big city 4-A high schools. On this day the Concert Choir scored right up there with the big schools. The choir director thought it appropriate to have an impromptu parade through town. She called the police and arranged for official emergency vehicles to meet us at the exit. Kids called their parents so they could join the parade. When the parade started we had a police car, an ambulance, two fire trucks, two busloads of choir kids, and about six family cars in the procession. The emergency vehicles ran their lights and sirens. The other bus driver and I blew our air horns to our hearts' content. The kids stuck their heads out the windows and cheered. Cars pulled over wondering what this was all about. Many honked their horns and cheered with us even though they didn't know what was going on. People stopped in the parking lots and stared. Some families quickly made up congratulation signs and filled balloons. They stood on the street corners to wave and yell. The police blocked traffic at the one stoplight in town. We made a ruckus and had the most fun on a school bus ever.

I'm just the bus driver. I'm not a part of the clubs, classes, and teams that these kids and their teachers and coaches are. I just haunt the edges of these events like a ghost observing life after his own is over. But the life of the kids and the excitement of the events are strong enough that they spill outside the lines, and I get to bask in the glow. I'm just the bus driver, but that still makes me lucky.

26 - HE'S A MONSTER

A year ago, at a stop where I pick up a whole slew of cousins, a cousin I had never met before got on. He was going to kindergarten. His hair had been carefully combed. He wore a plaid shirt and new jeans. His outfit was pulled together by the cowboy boots on his feet. His face shone with excitement and anticipation. His brothers and sisters had been getting on this bus ever since he could remember. Now it was his turn. Alas, it only lasted two days.

On the first day I noticed that this cute little boy, John, had a self-amplified voice. John always spoke as if he were at a rock concert. The second thing I noticed was that he had a way of annoying the other kids in such a manner that they got physical with him. There are a lot of annoying kids on my bus, but I've never seen anyone with this young boy's skill. Ironically, he wasn't trying to be annoying. He was just excited to be with the other kids and couldn't keep his hands to himself. On the next morning a second grader who was large for his size got physical with John. They were in a seat directly behind me so I couldn't see what happened, but I heard his older fourth-grade sister intervene with "Stop it. You're hurting him." I thought, "Uh oh," and yelled some questions back, but apparently the incident was over.

When John didn't get on the next morning his sister told me that he wouldn't be riding any more. His father brought the brothers and sisters to the bus a few days later. He came to the bus door and rather embarrassedly told me that John just wasn't ready to ride the bus yet. He said they had a little more work to do. I learned later that

John also got suspended from kindergarten for biting another boy's finger. Apparently the other boy stuck his finger in John's mouth and John decided that biting was the only way to remove it. It worked.

When John got on the bus on the first day of school this year I had misgivings. He looked pretty much the same as last year: plaid shirt, clean jeans, cowboy boots, and a look of excitement and anticipation on his face. Within about four seconds I learned that his voice was still self-amplified. By that afternoon I learned to give him the front passenger-side seat all to himself. He got along with others much better if there was space between him and them.

One day he wanted to show me what he brought to school. He unzipped his backpack and pulled out two full-sized rolling pins. "My teacher has playdough," he said, "but she doesn't have anything to work it with so I thought I'd help her out." I exclaimed on how helpful he was, but asked him to put them away. In his hands on the bus they wouldn't be rolling pins, but weapons, and most likely they would end up being turned on him.

Apparently John has a reputation in his own family. When he falls asleep on the fifty minute ride home, as he sometimes does, I've noticed that his sisters, who come up from the back of the bus, aren't in a hurry to wake him up. In fact a couple of times they left him and I had to wake him. I drove the high school volleyball team to a tournament and overheard some of the girls telling "top that" stories about their families. John's sister told the finger biting story. She ended with, "He's a monster."

Now that half the school year has gone by John and I are starting to come to an understanding. We even like each other a little. Don't get me wrong; I still have to exert quite a bit of energy to keep him in place, but his is a face I enjoy seeing each day. He likes the stories that I tell on the long run out to his stop. I've learned that green eggs and ham are his favorite breakfast foods. "They're delicious," he tells me. He was a cowboy for Halloween. He didn't think my idea of being a ballerina-cowboy (wear a tutu with his chaps) was a good idea.

Recently I played a little game with him. I offered him a candy bar if he could keep himself from touching the kids across the aisle from him or standing to see over the safety partition in front of him. Honestly, I didn't think he could do it. He did. Then he suffered through two days of disappointment when I forgot to bring the candy bar. On Friday I remembered. At his stop his high school sister, the one who called him a monster, got off the bus and waited by the door. John started to get off and then stopped.

"Oh, yeah, where's my candy bar?" he asked.

I had brought it but after thirteen other stops I had forgotten about it.

"Is it in here?" he grabbed the plastic grocery sack off the dash that, indeed, contained his candy bar. I nodded and he quickly reached in and pulled out his Twix.

"All right! Full size," he said as he clambered down the steps. His big sister glanced at me with a look of surprise and amusement on her face. Just before I shut the door I heard him say, in his amplified voice, "Don't worry. I'll share it with you." The last thing I saw as I pulled away was them holding hands as they began their quarter-mile walk up the hill to their home.

27 - GHOST BUS OF HIGHWAY 36

I drove the ninth grade football team to Grantsville the other day. We took the back route. That's about 120 miles of sagebrush valleys and tinder-dry hills on a narrow, two-lane highway. Traffic was minimal. In fact for most of those 120 miles my yellow school bus was the only thing moving for as far as you could see in either direction.

In the course of the journey we passed through or passed by several places that aren't much more than names on a map: Goshen, Eureka, Faust, and Bauer, to name a few. A couple of them actually appeared to have a population even if it was only five or six. Mostly they were just signs next to a lonely road with a place-name and an arrow pointing out into the sagebrush. Eureka is an old mining ghost town, except that people still live there. You don't drive through Eureka and fear the ghosts of old miners. It's the intermittent signs of living people that surprise you. One of those signs was a school crossing that still had a living crossing guard on duty as we drove by in the light, unexpected rain. At least I think she was living.

Eureka and Goshen are those types of small towns so hidden that they could be home to a cult that gives a human sacrifice at a secret ceremony once each year even though they are right in the middle of America. In reality they are probably a little piece of paradise away from the insanity of big city living. I know a fellow who used to live in Goshen and he seems legit.

As a school bus driver I'm attuned to the colors yellow and black. When I'm driving a bus and see those colors coming down the road I always think, "Ah, someone who understands." Imagine my surprise when out in the middle of nowhere I made out the back end of a school bus far ahead of me. I was traveling a little faster and slowly caught up. I wondered what this bus was doing so far out in the void. An active railroad line crossed the highway ahead of us. It was well-marked to alert drivers hypnotized by the long empty miles of the possibility of death if they didn't wake up. It was easy to see that the track was empty for ten miles in both directions, but this lonely bus in front of me turned on its hazard lights and came to a stop just like it was supposed to. I saw the doors open and the driver look both ways before she crossed the tracks. That's a good driver.

I passed the bus soon after and saw a few elementary age kids rush to the windows to look at us. They probably don't see many other buses during their ride. The bandana-wearing driver was looking up in her rearview mirror when I glanced over. No doubt she was telling the kids to sit down and be quiet. As far as I can tell she was on her regular route taking the kids home from school. Home must have been ranch houses scattered here and there throughout the sagebrush. I watched the bus for mile after mile as the distance between us slowly grew. Eventually, when I checked my mirrors, the bus was gone. Maybe it turned up one of those lonely roads next to a narrow sign with a place name and an arrow. Or maybe it was a ghost bus akin to the Flying Dutchman and had graced, or cursed, me with a sighting.

I looked for signs of the bus in the darkness of midnight on the return journey. I came to that desolate railroad crossing where we had both stopped. My flashing hazard lights reflected off the raised crossing bars. I opened my door to listen for trains . . . and maybe for the sound of another bus engine. Only one engine idled. With a sigh I shut my doors and drove my sleeping cargo home.

28 - THINGS I LIKE

I don't think I have met anyone who planned on being a bus driver when they grew up. Why would anyone want to? Most bus drivers end up in the job because they're in desperate need of a part-time job when a bus driving opening comes along. The pay is pretty good for a part-time job and the hours aren't bad. But driving a school bus isn't for everyone. Recently, in just one week, three "bad bus driver" stories hit the news. The bad behavior of the bus drivers in response to the bad behavior of the kids was appalling. Most of us bus drivers, when we hear these stories, usually don't rush to condemn. We don't try to excuse the drivers, either. Our response is tempered by the fact that we understand how the bus driver was feeling when he acted so badly. Perhaps we have had days where we stood close to the line that shouldn't be crossed and found the emotional resources to stay on the right side of it.

Most days are not like that. In fact almost every day there is at least one thing I like about being a school bus driver. For instance:

I like the kids. It's true that some kids are easier to like than others, but generally I like them all. I like the energy I feel from their youth. I like their laughter. I like their smiles. I like to read their t-shirts. I like to listen to their banter.

I like the way the five-year-old who sits behind the driver's seat will pat my head after I get my hair cut.

I like the way one six-year-old showed me her loose tooth and asked me to pull it. I respectfully declined.

I like the way kids will move to the front seat on the passenger side just to talk to me. The seat is left open for troublemakers who need a time out. Every once in a while I will look over to see a child I haven't called up sitting there. After a mile or two of silence they will call my name and start telling me a story from their life. They will continue to sit in that seat from anywhere between two days and a week and continue to talk to me. Then, when their need is over they will move back to their regular seat.

I like the way one precocious eight-year-old takes the time to show me her color-coordinated socks, pants, shirt, and hair bow. Sometimes there are even matching earrings.

I like the way some kids will sometimes stop and turn around when they get off the bus so they can wave to me. One boy often turns and says, "Thanks for the story." The look on his face is so sincere. At another stop the kids cut across a parking lot after I drop them off. I catch back up with them when I turn the corner. Sometimes they race me. They yell and wave when I honk the air horn.

I like the way the middle school girl stopped and sincerely thanked me before she got off the bus after I drove her back to the high school. She had fallen asleep in the back and awakened when I reached the elementary school across town.

I like the way the kids gently wake up a first grader who often falls asleep on the way to school. I have to hold his shoulder and steady him for a moment before he goes down the steps to make sure he's fully awake.

I like it when some of the older students take the time to respond to my greetings or questions with more color and energy than the usual grunt. One girl descended the steps then turned and spoke to me about her new hair cut (she thought it was too short). A boy took a moment to describe to me how Joe, their mule, can unlatch the gate to his corral with his lips. I actually saw Joe do this once. These unexpected, brief communications are always a pleasant surprise.

I like the playful laughter I hear from the back of the bus on the way to one of the last stops. It's coming from eight kids who are brothers and sisters and cousins. All the seats between me and them are empty. I can't hear what they are saying, only the fun energy they are saying it with. Often there is something one group is trying to grab from another group. Every once in a while it takes a few words over the intercom to get them back in their seats. Their happiness and fun fills the bus and I can't help smiling.

At the very last stop, four siblings get off and start up the gravel lane to their home. It's a half-mile walk. They range in age from fourteen to five years old. The five-year-old is the little sister. The others are her three big brothers. They are a beautiful sight as they start off down the lane side-by-side.

In-between all the "things I like" are the mundane, the annoying, and the downright irritating. But "the things I like" are tiny nuggets of gold lying among the gravel. The eye is drawn to the gold and the gravel is easily forgotten.

ABOUT THE AUTHOR

Before he gave up on being practical and normal Tory spent fifteen years in the high tech industry traveling the world. During these years he and his wife, Barbara, had eight children. Tory could often be seen busing his family around in a tan minivan. Driving a school bus was the next, inevitable step. In addition to *Bus Driver Diaries*, Tory has written two YA novels, *Joey and the Magic Map* and *Jacob and Lace*. If you like the books Tory writes feel free to leave a book review on Amazon.com and Goodreads.com. Tory currently lives with his wife and children in Levan, Utah, a lovely spot where you can still see the Milky Way.

21729886R00060

Printed in Poland
by Amazon Fulfillment
Poland Sp. z o.o., Wrocław